MICHAEL CRICHTON

Recent Title in
Critical Companions to Popular Contemporary Writers
Kathleen Gregory Klein, Series Editor

Mary Higgins Clark: A Critical Companion
Linda C. Pelzer

MICHAEL CRICHTON

A Critical Companion

Elizabeth A. Trembley

CRITICAL COMPANIONS TO POPULAR CONTEMPORARY WRITERS
Kathleen Gregory Klein, Series Editor

Greenwood Press
Westport, Connecticut • London

To Katie and Alec

Library of Congress Cataloging-in-Publication Data

Trembley, Elizabeth A. (Elizabeth Ann).
    Michael Crichton : a critical companion / Elizabeth A. Trembley.
      p. cm.—(Critical companions to popular contemporary
writers, ISSN 1082–4979)
    Includes bibliographical references and index.
    ISBN 0–313–29414–3 (alk. paper)
    1. Crichton, Michael—Criticism and interpretation. 2. Literature
and technology—United States—History—20th century. 3. Detective
and mystery stories, American—History and criticism. 4. Medicine
in literature. I. Title. II. Series.
PS3553.R48Z8 1996
813'.54—dc20   95–503

British Library Cataloguing in Publication Data is available.

Library of Congress Catalog Card Number: 95–503
ISBN: 0–313–29414–3
ISSN: 1082–4979

First published in 1996

Greenwood Press, 88 Post Road West, Westport, CT 06881
An imprint of Greenwood Publishing Group, Inc.

Printed in the United States of America

The paper used in this book complies with the
Permanent Paper Standard issued by the National
Information Standards Organization (Z39.48–1984).

10 9 8 7 6 5 4 3 2

ADVISORY BOARD

Contents

Contents

Series Foreword

The authors who appear in the series Critical Companions to Popular Contemporary Writers are all best-selling writers. They do not have only one successful novel, but a string of them. Fans, critics, and specialist readers eagerly anticipate their next book. For some, high cash advances and breakthrough sales figures are automatic; movie deals often follow. Some writers become household names, recognized by almost everyone.

But novels are read one by one. Each reader chooses to start and, more importantly, to finish a book because of what she or he finds there. The real test of a novel is in the satisfaction its readers experience. This series acknowledges the extraordinary involvement of readers and writers in creating a best-seller.

The authors included in this series were chosen by an Advisory Board composed of High School English teachers and High School and Public librarians. They ranked a list of best-selling writers according to their popularity among different groups of readers. Writers in the top-ranked group who had not received book-length, academic, literary analysis (or none in at least the past ten years) were chosen for the series. Because of this selection method, Critical Companions to Popular Contemporary Writers meets a need that is not addressed elsewhere.

The volumes in the series are written by scholars with particular expertise in analyzing popular fiction. These specialists add an academic focus on their best-selling writers to the popular success that these writers already enjoy.

The series is designed to appeal to a wide range of readers. The general reading public will find explanations for the appeal of these well-known writers. Fans will find biographical and fictional questions answered. Students will find literary analysis, discussions of fictional genres, carefully organized introductions to new ways of reading the novels, and bibliographies for additional research. Students will also be able to apply what they have learned from this book to their readings of future novels by these best-selling writers.

Each volume begins with a biographical chapter drawing on published information, autobiographies or memoirs, prior interviews, and, in some cases, interviews given especially for this series. A chapter on literary history and genres describes how the author's work fits into a larger literary context. The following chapters analyze the writer's most important, most popular, and most recent novels in detail. Each chapter focuses on a single novel. This approach, suggested by the Advisory Board as the most useful to student research, allows for an in-depth analysis of the writer's fiction. Close and careful readings with numerous examples show readers exactly how the novels work. These chapters are organized around three central elements: plot development (how the story line moves forward), character development (what the reader knows about the important figures), and theme (the significant ideas of the novel). Chapters may also include sections on generic conventions (how the novel is similar to or different from others in its same category of science fiction, fantasy, thriller, etc.), narrative point of view (who tells the story and how), symbols and literary language, and historical or social context. Each chapter ends with an "alternative reading" of the novel. The volume concludes with a primary and secondary bibliography, including reviews.

The Alternative Readings are a unique feature of this series. By demonstrating a particular way of reading each novel, they provide a clear example of how a specific perspective can reveal important aspects of the book. In each alternative reading section, one contemporary literary theory—such as feminist criticism, Marxism, new historicism, deconstruction, or Jungian psychological critique is defined in brief, easily comprehensible language. That definition is then applied to the novel to highlight specific features that might go unnoticed or be understood differently in a more general reading of the novel. Each volume defines two or three specific theories, making them part of the reader's understanding of how diverse meanings may be constructed from a single novel.

Taken collectively, the volumes in the Critical Companions to Popular Contemporary Writers series provide a wide-ranging investigation of the complexities of current best-selling fiction. By treating these novels seriously as both literary works and publishing successes, the series demonstrates the potential of popular literature in contemporary culture.

Kathleen Gregory Klein
Southern Connecticut State University

Acknowledgments

While writing a book is never easy, living with someone who writes a book can be unexpectedly difficult. The exasperation and exhaustion, the truncated weekends, the panicked requests for help, the time given too reluctantly, the vacant expression during dinners—only heroes can meet these writer's quirks with encouragement and love. I have been blessed with friends and family of remarkable patience and ability, both of which I used mightily. Diane Kooiker spent countless hours searching out texts. Bill Reynolds willingly proofed every word of this volume, even over holidays. Kathy Klein reassured at all the right moments. Morgan, Baker, and Friday insisted on the daily beach walks which kept me sane. And finally, thankfully, the enthusiasm of my family and friends reminded me how much fun this really is.

1

The Life of Michael Crichton

"I was an urban, technological man accustomed to making things happen. . . . anything less implied shameful passivity" (*Travels*, 152). Author Michael Crichton has lived a life full of continuing and often astonishing accomplishment. He has taken control and made things happen. Born on October 23, 1942, in Chicago, Illinois, John Michael Crichton (pronounced Cry-ton) grew up on Long Island, New York. The eldest of four children, he earned his A.B. degree summa cum laude in 1964 from Harvard University. He put himself through Harvard Medical School by writing paperback thrillers on weekends and completed his M.D. in 1969. Before leaving medicine for writing, he worked as a postdoctoral fellow at the Salk Institute for Biological Studies from 1969 to 1970. He has hiked in jungles and dived on wrecks. He has bent spoons in psychic experiments. And he has written the novel that was made into the largest grossing movie of all time. Crichton has been married four times and currently lives in California with his wife Anne-Marie Martin and his daughter Taylor. He has won the Edgar Award from the Mystery Writers of America twice, for *A Case of Need* in 1968 and for *The Great Train Robbery* in 1979. Crichton was also named Writer of the Year in 1970 by the Association of American Medical Writers for one of his full-length nonfiction studies, *Five Patients: A Hospital Explained* (1970). Currently over 21 million copies of his books are in print.

Most people take a lifetime to master a career in medicine, or writing fiction, or directing movies. But Michael Crichton has succeeded at all of these. This remarkable man enjoys a variety of interests, and his curiosity drives him to excel at all of them. This chapter discusses five of the most important influences on his writing in the order in which they developed (though they do overlap chronologically in some cases). From childhood, through medical school, while directing movies, during travels around the world, and in exploration of the unexplained powers of the mind, Crichton has made things happen and grown as a writer.

The first major influence on Crichton's writing is his pre-professional life. This includes his childhood and undergraduate college experiences. His remarkable interest in diverse areas and his writing ability have their seeds in his childhood. Crichton's parents continually encouraged him to pursue whatever interested him. "It was an idea in my family that it was good to have an interest in many diverse things—that you didn't have to have a scheme whereby it all fit together" ("Michael Crichton," *Current Biography*, 1993, 11). One of the things Crichton loved was the construction and observation of technology, which clearly shows in his works today. His brother Douglas remembers, "Michael was always out in the backyard with a telescope he had built, looking at the sky" (Chambers, 96). At the same time, Crichton loved the fantasy of film. He fondly remembers seeing *To Catch a Thief* with his parents. "Here was this magic movie," he remarked. "It was funny and exciting and I loved it" (Chambers, 96). "When I was growing up, I didn't want to be a character out of Hemingway; I wanted to be Cary Grant" (B. Rose, 226). This no doubt influenced the construction of his characters and the visual, cinematic style that has become Crichton's hallmark.

More than anything else, however, Crichton wanted to become a professional writer (*Travels*, 77). Before he left elementary school, he had written a script for a puppet show and long stories ("Michael Crichton," *Current Biography*, 1976, 186). At home, family dinner conversations often focused on writing. Crichton's father, a corporate president and former editor of *Advertising Age*, valued concise, clear composition. Crichton believes this inspired three of the four children to publish books (*Travels*, 78). Encouraged by his father, the fourteen-year-old Crichton submitted a travel article based on a family vacation to the *New York Times*. To his surprise, it was accepted. Inspired, Crichton wrote and submitted many more articles to a variety of publications in the following three years. None was published.

Crichton seems to have felt not only inspired, but *driven* to achieve. He wanted to avoid "shameful passivity" and ridicule. Crichton's father did not just encourage his son, however. He could act harshly, even violently, and this caused considerable tension in the household. Though Crichton at times hated his father (*Travels*, 193), he ultimately felt sadness because his father often concealed positive emotions like love and respect (*Travels*, 194). The pain of that unresolved relationship influenced Crichton for decades.

Crichton also suffered as an adolescent because of his extreme height. He had grown to an awkward six feet, seven inches by the time he was thirteen years old. Other children teased him, but he determined to get back at them all through use of his intelligence (Gross, 130). Crichton eventually reached six feet, nine inches in height, which later granted him a remarkable presence on movie sets and during interviews.

When he enrolled at Harvard University, Crichton intended to pursue his love for writing and major in English. He changed his mind, however, when he received C grades on his work. Crichton could not believe that he really only performed at an "average" level, especially after all of his father's lessons. So he tested the Harvard grading system by submitting under his own name an essay written by George Orwell (author of *Animal Farm* and *1984*). When Orwell's essay got a B−, Crichton decided to study anthropology and premed instead. Eventually his interest in science and the chance to help people led the young man to become a physician (*Travels*, 4).

This portion of his life influenced Crichton's writing in more general than specific ways. Though his autobiography, *Travels*, does discuss his childhood, his other works do not. However, his parents' encouragement of a wide range of interests set the stage for him to write knowledgeably about alien viruses, computer implants in human brains, medieval Vikings, Victorian train robberies, undersea habitats, cloning, and international economics—to name only a few of his topics. His troubled relationship with his father and his extraordinary height strengthened him to handle opposition, and probably honed the sense of conflict contained in his plots.

Medical school, which Crichton began in 1964 and completed in 1969, provided the second major influence on his life and writing. His experiences shaped the attitudes toward science and scientists that he later presented in much of his fiction. At every level, Crichton found the community of future doctors riddled with emotional tension. While the rest of his experience at Harvard focused on the pursuit of knowledge, medical studies were different. Here students competed with each other in a hostile environment. In his autobiography, Crichton condemns in detail the lack of attention the medical school curriculum paid to training doctors to be compassionate. He describes his own experience as a hazing, not an education. For instance, during the first year, the uncomfortable medical students coped with their human dissection work by making jokes and teasing. Once they even played a laboratory football game with human livers (*Travels*, 10). Crichton disliked the situation, but he survived (though with the dubious honor of being the student who set the most fires during chemistry lab—once even scorching the laboratory ceiling) (*Travels*, 4).

Crichton's first rotation in neurology continued to reveal the emotional failings of this supposedly caring community. His autobiography reveals that there he observed the chief resident routinely sticking pins in patients in a sadistic test of consciousness (*Travels*, 30). Some younger residents regularly began their shifts by getting high on dope, unafraid because no one ever noticed (*Travels*, 27). In the obstetrics ward, righteous nurses often refused to give the unwed mothers painkillers. Crichton felt he had entered Dante's *Inferno*. There the women were "all twisting and writhing in rubber-sheeted beds . . . all shrieking at the top of their lungs in the most hideous agony" (*Travels*, 48). His experiences gave him a belief about scientists that would later appear in many of his novels: "How a doctor behaved was at least as important as what he knew" (*Travels*, 12). This is evident in *The Terminal Man*, *Sphere*, and *Jurassic Park*. It also shaped Crichton's development of the enormously successful television series "ER," which debuted in 1994. Crichton's medical education also gave him a knowledge of scientific experimentation, medical practices, and psychology, subjects he dealt with in *The Terminal Man*, *Congo*, *Sphere*, *Disclosure*, and other novels.

Ironically, it was after Crichton abandoned his English major to pursue medicine that he began to publish on a regular basis. Knowing that Ian Fleming's James Bond novels had achieved tremendous popularity, Crichton decided to write similar books (*Travels*, 79). He wrote his first thriller, *Odds On*, at age twenty-three under the pseudonym John Lange. Over the next five years, Crichton wrote a total of ten novels on weekends and on vacations, sometimes churning out 10,000 words each day ("Michael Crichton," *Current Biography*, 1976, 184). These novels appeared under several pseudonyms. Under the name John Lange he wrote *Odds On* (1966), *Scratch One* (1967), *Easy Go* (1968), *Zero Cool* (1969), *The Venom Business* (1969), *Drug of Choice* (1970), *Grave Descend* (1970), and *Binary* (1971). *A Case of Need* (1968) appeared under the pseudonym Jeffrey Hudson, a name the six foot, nine inch Crichton borrowed from a famous seventeenth-century dwarf ("Michael Crichton," *Current Biogra-*

phy, 1976, 185). This novel was influenced by Crichton's experience as a medical student at Boston Lying In Hospital. He even co-wrote one novel with his brother Douglas, *Dealing: Or, The Berkeley-to-Boston Forty-Brick Lost-Bag Blues* (1971), under the name Michael Douglas. All of these novels except *A Case of Need*, which was reissued under Crichton's own name in early 1994, have gone out of print and are extremely difficult to find. Because most were issued as paperback originals, copies that libraries did own have long since disappeared.

Ultimately, the success of his weekend writing helped tempt the disillusioned young medical student away from the medical profession. In 1969, the gap between schooling and his success as a writer widened. That year, the Mystery Writers of America named *A Case of Need* best novel of the previous year. The immense popularity of *The Andromeda Strain* (1969) further lured Crichton away from medicine. Finally Crichton realized that his "other life" had begun to interfere with his performance as a medical student. He listened to patients with an ear to how he could use their stories in a book. Knowing that he was not behaving like a doctor that he would want to consult, he decided to quit (*Travels*, 74).

The final push to leave medicine came when the twenty-six-year-old Crichton experienced numbness in his right arm for several weeks, eventually accompanied by tingling in his legs. Several of Harvard's best doctors diagnosed multiple sclerosis. This made Crichton realize that if he only had a few years of activity left, then writing was his top priority (*Travels*, 87). Since then he has had no further attacks, and to this day he is uncertain whether he experienced a single attack of MS or an anxiety reaction to abandoning his medical career.

His colleagues at Harvard thought his decision to leave medicine unrealistic at best (*Travels*, 87). However, when people found out that he had written *The Andromeda Strain* and sold it to the movies for a substantial sum, they encouraged him. This insincerity bothered him (*Travels*, 87). He determined that he would complete his M.D., then leave the medical profession.

Knowing that he would try to become a professional writer, Crichton spent his final rotation examining patients' emotions about their illnesses (*Travels*, 60). His observations eventually led to his first extended work of nonfiction, *Five Patients: A Hospital Explained*. During this time, Crichton first realized that most patients accepted a connection between their mental processes and their physical health. He began to wonder about the importance of psychological factors in causing disease. This notion of the spiritual affecting the physical drove Crichton's later investigations into psychic phenomena.

Following graduation from medical school in 1969, Crichton went to Europe for a year on a travel fellowship, where he spent some time teaching anthropology at Cambridge and traveling on the continent. He returned to the United States and accepted a position at the prestigious Salk Institute for Biological Studies in California. The move to the West Coast also brought with it the third major influence on Crichton's writing: the opportunity to make movies. Crichton had never really lost this childhood desire. Even at his medical school entrance interview, he had said that if he weren't applying to medical school, he'd like to become a movie director (B. Rose, 220).

Over the next seven years, Crichton continued to write successful novels. But he also began to explore the world of film, making four of his seven feature films. Crichton felt that his medical training helped him develop as a director. Applying the medical school method of learning to filmmaking, Crichton observed experienced practitioners in action until he could perform the operation on his own. In 1970 Crichton observed director Robert Wise filming *The Andromeda Strain*. In early 1972 he observed the filming of two more of his novels, *Dealing* by Paul Williams and *The Carey Treatment* (from *A Case of Need*) by Blake Edwards. Crichton then decided that he, too, could direct a film. He negotiated his directorial debut into the film rights of his next novel. Later in 1972 he directed the made-for-television movie of his novel *Binary*. The first theatrical film he directed was *Westworld*, from his own original script, in 1973. Crichton's next two films also met with critical acclaim. *Coma* (1978) was a medical thriller based on Robin Cook's novel. *The Great Train Robbery* (1979) was based on Crichton's own novel. These led critics to claim that Crichton "promises to be one of the most exciting new talents in American film" (B. Rose, 220).

Crichton believed his success grew from his experiences.

> As a medical student, you were always tired, but you had to perform anyhow. . . . Medicine is really terrific at teaching you to acquire new skills fast. . . . You also learn a lack of embarrassment at not knowing how to do something. . . . Medicine also got you into the frame of mind of dealing with very high-pressure situations, dealing with complex factors, emergencies. You often had to make fast decisions. Something is always going wrong in a movie, and that kind of experience

is invaluable in salvaging a situation. Direction is really hard work. (B. Rose, 224)

In response to his early success, the media quickly became fascinated with Crichton as an unpretentious boy wonder who seemed to master every task he touched. *Vogue* assessed Crichton as "a very nice person . . . an obviously brilliant but otherwise not unusual young man involved in acquiring, assimilating, and processing great quantities of information at an incredible rate" (B. Rose, 186). Another interviewer described him as "rosy, curly, scrubbed, tall as a chimney . . . whose bouncy, outspoken chat, bloomy youth, and loose-jointed energy are as misleading as an advanced nuclear device sewn into Raggedy Andy" (Robinson, 100). Regarding his early success, Crichton is not so glib. "I don't believe in luck. I worked harder than anybody I know—literally, day and night" (Sauter, 22–23). Hard work and the desire to make things happen, not the Midas touch, brought him his success.

This experience with film sharpened Crichton's ability to write novels that would appeal to Hollywood. This was a major ingredient in the success of his later books *Jurassic Park*, *Rising Sun*, and *Disclosure*. They are extremely cinematic in their presentation, focusing on visual elements that let readers see the action like little movies in their minds. Crichton has even joked about the influence of film on his writing. When working on *Jurassic Park*, he told people he was "writing the most expensive movie ever made" (Gross, 129). And he was right.

Unfortunately, the last three films Crichton directed—shot between 1981 and 1989—did not find the same critical or popular success as *Westworld* and *The Great Train Robbery*. *Looker* (1981) was called a "disappointing comedy melo-drama" (*Current Biography*, 1993, 12) and "Crichton's only certifiable flop" (Sauter, 23). In response, Crichton remarked, "No one was making the movie they wanted to make. . . . They make it so you're responsible for it but you can't control it" (Sauter, 23). *Runaway* (1984) confounded critics with plot inconsistencies. Critical comments beginning, "It's hard to imagine why a smart guy like Crichton does dumb things like . . . " (Kroll, 84) clustered about the film. Even *Physical Evidence* (1989) met with disdain. *Variety* called this "a box-office belly-flop . . . it's really anybody's guess as to what's going on, since the film's so choppily assembled. . . . Director Michael Crichton certainly used to be able to tell a pretty good suspense yarn (*Westworld* and *Coma* attest to that), but muddled storytelling here leaves loose ends not only as to whodunit but why" ("Film Reviews," 14).

In late 1994, a film-related project that Crichton had tried to sell to television for nearly twenty years finally appeared. Crichton created and co-produced the NBC series *ER*, using his own experiences as a resident in an emergency ward. This series emphasizes Crichton's interest in the emotional capabilities of the physicians, as well as their technical expertise. The show rocketed to success, attracting over 30 million viewers each week in its first season ("Michael Crichton and John Wells").

Crichton could not be satisfied with performances that brought rejection, criticism, or bad reviews. Ultimately filmmaking proved to be too uncertain a field. Perhaps if he had pursued directing as a sole occupation he could have found more success, but even as he began developing this new trade he continued to write. In 1973 Warner Brothers rejected his script for *The Terminal Man* because he had departed too extensively from his own novel. This began an inward spiraling of anxiety over the direction Crichton wanted his life to take. At thirty he had money and celebrity, but also a divorce and lawsuits (Sauter, 23). Unsettled by his dissatisfaction with success, he started psychiatric counseling and discovered yet another new interest in his life: travel.

From 1976 through 1980, Crichton published no new novels. Instead he devoted himself to travel, the fourth major influence on his writing. He traveled beyond the usual tourist places, into the exotic, the uncomfortable, and the challenging. Travel helped Crichton discover new aspects of the world which permeate his later fiction. For instance, on his first trip to Thailand, his encounter with Buddhism helped him realize how intensely culture-bound he was. He learned how immersion in only one culture handicapped his interactions with others, despite his best intentions. He found the social and religious rules of Buddhism mystifying, and despite his honest attempts, almost impossible not to break (*Travels*, 119). For instance, because of his great height Crichton struggled constantly to keep his head lower than the head on the statue of Buddha in people's homes (*Travels*, 117). His experiences inspired him to travel extensively into more foreign cultures to find out what he had been missing.

Soon the observant writer realized that he traveled to discover more about the hidden and untried elements of his self. Crichton developed "an almost obsessive desire for experiences that would increase [his] self-awareness" (*Travels*, 384). One critic connects that personal growth to Crichton's fiction. "His travels have forced him to deal with his fears; a motif that runs through his fiction" (Sauter, 24). Over a period of several years, Crichton faced many frightening obstacles. He climbed Mt. Kilimanjaro, bloodying his feet all the way up to the ankles. He dove with a group of hundreds of sharks off a New Zealand coral reef and explored sunken ships. He hiked through exotic jungles and stood his ground while a mammoth silverback gorilla charged him in rage.

Crichton's experiences with other cultures taught him much about American culture. He argues that contemporary culture has conditioned us to fear direct experience by filtering all our thoughts and attitudes. "One of the most difficult features of direct experience is that it is unfiltered by any theories and expectations. It's hard to observe without imposing a theory to explain what we're seeing ... it takes an enormous effort to ... just experience directly.... It's surprising what you can learn that way" (*Travels*, 388–389).

Crichton's travels influenced all of his subsequent novels in some way. His adventures in Asia and Africa and under the ocean's surface contributed to the settings of novels like *Sphere, Congo, Jurassic Park*, and *Rising Sun*. His new perspectives on American culture influenced themes in *Rising Sun* and *Disclosure*. His experience as a visitor in an unfamiliar world helped him develop characterization in *Congo, Sphere, Rising Sun*, and *Disclosure*. *Congo* in particular contains details from Crichton's experiences in Africa, including mountain climbing and encountering gorillas.

Love of such direct experience also brought this Harvard-trained medical doctor into contact with psychic powers, the fifth of the important influences on Crichton's life and work. Crichton talks very little about this aspect of his life in interviews. "When you start talking about some of this, people start thinking you're some kind of New Age loony" (Sauter, 24). However, his experiences in the last fifteen years have changed many of his attitudes about life. While working on the film of *The Great Train Robbery* in London in 1979, Crichton began to visit the Spiritualist Association of Great Britain. He wanted to explore his old medical school interest in the powers of the mind and its effect on health and success. At the association, he consulted a psychic for ten dollars an hour. Intrigued, Crichton went almost every day after work for several weeks, visiting many different spiritualists (*Travels*, 208). He entered every reading intent on objectively evaluating the success of the psychics' practice. He refused to give any clues, verbal or nonverbal, that could provide subtle help. The accurate readings that many of the psychics gave convinced him that *something* was happening, though he wasn't sure what. He felt he must learn more.

Crichton continued to seek out psychic experiences for over a decade after these initial encounters in England. At a workshop in the early 1980s, Crichton observed and experienced many traditionally inexplicable events, from the powerful laying on of hands, to seeing auras, to "hearing" a cactus speak. At these amazing events, Crichton panicked. He could not explain what he knew to be true. "I didn't think I was crazy. . . . Something cracked in my way of looking at things" (*Travels*, 281–282). Ultimately he realized that his own prejudices and fears had held him back. In 1985 Crichton's spiritual travels continued when he learned to bend spoons using psychic energy. Having done that, however, he found it unremarkable, no magic trick. Such boredom often occurs, he writes, after mastering a so-called psychic experience (*Travels*, 355–356).

Nevertheless, Crichton does occasionally worry that his investigations into psychic realms have taken him too far from rational, intellectual tradition. One day, in a test to assess his own gullibility, Crichton summarized all the points these experiences had taught him, and was surprised to find only three:

1. Consciousness has legitimate dimensions not yet guessed at.
2. At least some psychic phenomena are real.
3. There are energies associated with the human body that are not yet understood.

These beliefs were not so very different, Crichton felt, from those of Carl Jung and William James (*Travels*, 382–384). It was simply a balance between the rational and the intuitive. Crichton has maintained a cautious rationality about his experiences, but insists on their importance and validity.

In particular, Crichton likes to cite the example of how one psychic experience affected his relationship with his father, who had died several years earlier. While experimenting with out-of-body phenomena, Crichton says, his consciousness visited the astral plain, where he met with the spirit of his father. He experienced tremendous initial anxiety because of the unhappy nature of their past relationship. However, that passed when the spirit suddenly embraced him. "In that instant of embrace, I saw and felt everything in my relationship with my father . . . all the love that was there between us, and all the confusion and misunderstanding that had overpowered it. . . . My relationship with my father had been resolved in a flash" (*Travels*, 340–342). The clash of this sort of experience with his technical, scientific training has not escaped Crichton. He continues to explore the combination of science and the mind's power.

Crichton wrote about the interaction of science and the power of the human mind in *The Terminal Man*, in the discussions of chaos theory in *Jurassic Park*, and in his focus on the development of virtual reality technology in *Disclosure*. But Crichton focused on it most significantly in his 1987 novel, *Sphere*, where scientists, armed with the most up-to-date technology, must battle monsters created from their own imaginations.

Recently, Crichton's life has become much more traditional. His fourth marriage continues solidly and has produced his only child, a daughter, Taylor. He lives with his family in California in a house he calls "conventional," full of "family and art work" ("Conventional Wisdom," 102). Earlier in his life, Crichton lived in a canyon-top house with "glassed pavilions, reflecting pools, and groomed lawns suggest[ing] a Japanese tranquillity" (B. Rose, 186). In contrast to this showplace, Crichton likes the used feel of his current home. Since moving there, "nothing has been done. Not even minor cosmetic changes. My office at home has a bare light bulb in the ceiling . . . three years later the bare bulb is still there" ("Conventional Wisdom," 101). About his new conventional life, Crichton remarks, "Living in a house for show is like wearing shoes that always pinch. What's the point?" At his house "you can put your feet up on all the tables and chairs. You can put glasses on all the surfaces. No worrying about wet rings or scratches" (102).

Crichton's daily schedule is equally normal. He does most of his writing at an office not far from his house, usually from 6 A.M until 4 P.M., returning home for lunch. The family dines regularly at 6.30 P.M. because Crichton likes "to eat dinner in daylight" (102). Crichton enjoys diving, tennis, movies, and fast cars. He reads about three hundred books a year ("Michael Crichton," *Current Biography*, 1976, 186). He doesn't know how to play most games and finds spectator sports dull ("Conventional Wisdom," 101). Crichton and his wife don't go out much. "It seems to us that family life is important, and we find most socializing lifeless and mundane" (102).

With a portion of his earnings, Crichton has collected both modern and primitive art. In the early 1980s his art collection was exhibited at several universities in Southern California. Crichton's love of art led to his first extended work of nonfiction since *Five Patients. Jasper Johns*, a monograph on the work of the contemporary American artist, accompanied a retrospective exhibit of Johns's works at the Whitney Museum

in New York in 1977. Johns himself selected Crichton to write the catalogue, hoping that it would become something other than the usual sterile commentary. One critic argues that Crichton failed this challenge,
however, precisely because of his writing techniques. He relies very
heavily on genre models in his fiction and did so here, in effect producing an art catalogue that did not develop the new style commentary that
Johns desired (Alloway, 571).

Crichton's other two excursions into nonfiction came in 1985 and 1988.
In 1985 he wrote a computer guide for the average person. It explained
simply and clearly everything from turning on a machine to how random
access memory operates. *Electronic Life* explained computers "and why
we shouldn't fear the new machine" (Sauter, 23). Crichton believes that
"just as computers have changed his own work life, they will change the
very existence of almost everyone else" ("A How-to for Have-nots").
Critics praised this book for its common sense, its practical approaches,
its soothing and sympathetic tone. At about the same time, Crichton
worked with a programmer to produce a computer game called *Amazon*.
This was a piece of "interactive fiction," an attempt to "tell a story in a
new way" (Staples, 26).

Crichton's final nonfiction adventure is *Travels* (1988). This autobiography examines in depth his medical school, world traveling, and psychic experiences. Anyone interested in understanding more about this
complex and accomplished individual should read this book. Its wry
self-examination and good humor entertain as its human insights provide further background for understanding Crichton's novels. Here
Crichton brings together the vast variety of his experience and tries to
construct a life philosophy for himself. He urges his readers to do the
same for themselves.

Thus far, life has taught Michael Crichton that lasting pleasure comes
from "a sense of connectedness with others, some measure of control
over one's life, total absorption in meaningful activity and doing new
things" (Crichton, "Happiness," 90). And certainly he has done all of
this. No author has connected with a larger audience. His works have
touched almost everyone in American society through print or film.
Crichton is "one of Hollywood's most valuable literary properties" ("Michael Crichton," *Current Biography*, 1993, 10) because of the way his novels lend themselves to cinematic adaptation. In 1993 he became "the first
living novelist to have two novels in circulation as hit movies in the same
year" ("Michael Crichton," *Current Biography*, 1993, 14). Following the
success of the films *Jurassic Park* and *Rising Sun*, Crichton was paid $3.5

million for the film rights to *Disclosure*. Such a connection with his contemporary audience grants Crichton financial control over his life and creative control over future film developments of his fictions.

Throughout a life full of childhood interests, medical school, film directing, world travels, and psychic experimentation, Crichton has constantly devoted himself to new and meaningful activities. When asked in 1981 if he regretted giving up the humane values of medicine, Crichton responded, "Helping people is a very tenuous concept. I think what I'm doing is socially useful. People need the mirrors of experience they find in books and movies. They want to feel they're not alone. People undervalue movie directors and overvalue doctors. One is as good as another" (Chambers, 98). A safe statement from the man who has succeeded at both—and much more.

2

Michael Crichton's Literary Heritage

During his career, Michael Crichton has published many kinds of writing, including novels, computer manuals, monographs on modern art, social essays, short stories, and film screenplays. Similarly, his twenty-two novels (published under his own name as well as several pseudonyms) stretch over several popular genres. Though critics consider Crichton primarily a writer of science fiction because of novels like *The Andromeda Strain* and *Jurassic Park*, his work also encompasses detective fiction, the adventure novel, and gothic fiction. In addition, many critics credit Crichton with inventing the "techno-thriller," a novel which blends technology, suspense, and hot social issues. Through this variety of approaches to fiction, Crichton has ensured his longevity in the American popular literature marketplace.

This chapter, and the remainder of this book, will focus on the work for which Crichton is best known, the nine novels originally published under his own name that have entertained millions of readers. All remain in print. Crichton's earlier pseudonymous fiction is less well known, in part because it is a less mature, less carefully crafted effort. Also, most of these novels appeared as paperback originals and are currently extremely difficult to locate. Of these, only *A Case of Need* has returned to print under Crichton's own name.

Several popular genres intertwine within Crichton's work. Therefore, an understanding of their interrelated development provides insight into

Crichton's fiction. This chapter investigates the history of gothic, detective, adventure, and science fiction novels, focusing on their stylistic and thematic characteristics. The fifty-year period from 1865 to 1915 represents the blossoming of popular literature in the Anglo-American world. A list of some of the most successful and influential texts in gothic, detective, adventure, and science fiction illustrates the clustering within these dates:

Mary Shelley	*Frankenstein*	1818
Lewis Caroll	*Alice's Adventures in Wonderland*	1865
Jules Verne	*20,000 Leagues Under the Sea*	1869
H. Rider Haggard	*King Solomon's Mines*	1885
R. L. Stevenson	*Dr. Jekyll and Mr. Hyde*	1886
Arthur Conan Doyle	*Study in Scarlet*	1887
Arthur Conan Doyle	*The White Company*	1891
H. G. Wells	*The Time Machine*	1895
H. G. Wells	*The Island of Dr. Moreau*	1896
Bram Stoker	*Dracula*	1897
H. G. Wells	*The War of the Worlds*	1898
Arthur Conan Doyle	*The Hound of the Baskervilles*	1902
Arthur Conan Doyle	*The Lost World*	1912
Edgar Rice Burroughs	*Tarzan of the Apes*	1914

The terrific success of these authors influenced all popular fiction writers who followed them, including Michael Crichton. The second section of this chapter considers Crichton's works in the context of this heritage.

THE DEVELOPMENT OF POPULAR GENRES

Gothic Fiction

Gothic—or horror—fiction has tortured delighted readers with daytime frights and sleepless nights for over two centuries. The genre, which began with Horace Walpole's *The Castle of Otranto* in 1764, rose to popularity with novels such as Ann Radcliffe's *The Mysteries of Udolpho* (1794) and Matthew Lewis's *The Monk* (1796). It grew ever more shocking from Mary Shelley's *Frankenstein* (1818) to Bram Stoker's *Dracula* (1897). In the twentieth century, gothic fiction has continued in the works of contemporary horror authors like Stephen King and V. C. Andrews. Gothic horror has filled the screens in countless movie houses. Gothic has also given birth to the social melodrama. Emotionally charged, these family sagas provide "a detailed, intimate, and realistic analysis of major social or historical phenomena" (Cawelti, 261). These authors usually treat their social settings critically. They focus on secrecy and wickedness, but ultimately work out an ending in which the sympathetic characters triumph. Colleen McCullough's *The Thorn Birds* is an outstanding example of this type of novel.

The style and themes developed in gothic fiction, though familiar to us now, broke new ground in the eighteenth and nineteenth centuries. Stylistically, gothic tales brought to popular fiction a new emotional intensity. Characters constantly experienced the heights of horror and happiness, and readers empathized with them. Conflicts between characters of terrific evil and angelic goodness held audiences' interest. Readers loved to wonder whether the heroes or heroines would survive with their virtue intact. Plots moved readers from one crisis to the next quickly so they could not put their books down. To further involve readers, writers of gothic stories created verisimilitude, or the appearance of truth through details. They presented their novels as actual reproductions of letters, diaries, maps, and speeches.

The thematic elements of gothic fiction are broad, but two had great influence on subsequent literature. The first is the inability of the individual to communicate or connect with his or her true self, other people, or nature. The second is the fragmented, irrational world that develops because communication is impossible. The presentation of letters and diaries in the novels mirrors this focus on a fragmented world. This loss of central stability leads some characters into irrational or even insane action. Other themes of gothic fiction include pursuit and confinement, the apparent superiority of evil, the failure of rationality and morality against that evil, and even supernatural encounters (Frank, 8–9). In the twentieth century, some gothic works out a lighter theme. Evil things happen, but only to people who brought the evil upon themselves (Cawelti, 262).

Perhaps the most important example of gothic fiction is Mary Shelley's *Frankenstein*, which not only rocketed the gothic genre to popularity, but also proved that scientific literature could entertain. In this tale, Dr. Frankenstein creates and then attempts to kill his own uncontrollable monster. Shelley grips readers in horrified suspense by presenting each character's tale in his own words and by drawing heavily on contemporary scientific theories about electricity. Frankenstein's world grows ever more chaotic and fragmented as his powerful genius fails to withstand the force of the monster he created.

In addition to writing an exciting piece of gothic fiction, Shelley stretched the genre. She combined the emotional intensity of gothic and the rationality of science literature with contemporary social concerns. She gave popular form to people's fears about the rapid advance of science in the early nineteenth century. People had begun to worry that the Industrial Revolution and the new fields of psychology and evolution would break down morality. They wondered if intellectual and technical "progress" could outstrip human moral evolution, making humans unable to control their own creations. *Frankenstein* presented a myth that became a mainstay of later gothic and science fiction as the two genres continued to intertwine. The spectacle of a creature fabricated by humans and technology, whose creator oversteps natural boundaries, lies at the center of many works, including *Dr. Jekyll and Mr. Hyde, The Island of Doctor Moreau*, and, of course, Crichton's *Jurassic Park*. In addition, the idea that the psychological elements of an individual personality could become dangerously real occurs frequently. We see it in *Frankenstein, Dr. Jekyll and Mr. Hyde, Dracula, The Picture of Dorian Gray*, and Crichton's own *The Terminal Man* and *Sphere*, to name a few.

These gothic elements appear throughout Crichton's novels. The social criticism of the melodrama forms the thematic center of each of his books. As later chapters illustrate, each of his novels focuses on a controversial social issue, examines it from a variety of perspectives, and clearly states Crichton's view of the situation. Perhaps the most interesting examples of this focus on social criticism occur in Crichton's latest books: *Jurassic Park, Rising Sun*, and *Disclosure*. Stylistically, Crichton draws from the gothic, especially in creating intense suspense for his readers. His plots move quickly between episodes, depicting actions with vivid detail and drawing readers into all of the novels. The most gothic of Crichton's novels is *Eaters of the Dead*. In it the mist monsters are supernatural creatures of astonishing evil. That book also takes the form of a diary, presenting a world seemingly fragmented into different social groups that have little understanding of each other.

Detective Fiction

Detective fiction is a direct descendent of gothic fiction in the fictional family tree. It was first made popular by the stories of Edgar Allan Poe and Arthur Conan Doyle, both of whom also wrote gothic tales of horror. For Poe, detective fiction began as a challenge of opposites. Immersed in fiction that focused on the apparent triumph of irrationality and evil, he sought a change. So he wrote three stories that pivoted on the supremacy of a totally rational character, Monsieur Dupin: "The Murders in the Rue Morgue" (1841), "The Mystery of Marie Roget" (1842), and "The Purloined Letter" (1845). Poe's stories inspired the not-so-successful physician Doyle, almost half a century later. Doyle modeled Sherlock Holmes and Dr. Watson on Dupin and his nameless sidekick. He even reworked plots from Poe's tales into mysteries for Holmes to solve. In turn, scores of detective fiction authors have used Doyle as a springboard for their own work, creating one of the most diverse and active genres of popular fiction. Detective fiction has provided readers with Agatha Christie's Jane Marple, Dorothy L. Sayers's Lord Peter Wimsey, Dashiell Hammett's Sam Spade, Ian Fleming's James Bond, and Sara Paretsky's V. I. Warshawski.

While they grew from the same stylistic and thematic roots, detective fiction ultimately turned gothic on its heels. Where gothic fiction emphasized emotional involvement in its characters by the reader, detective fiction created intellectual intensity. Suspense became not a matter of *whether* heroes would survive their adventures, but *how* they would outsmart the opponent. When a mystery presented itself in detective fiction, rationality and morality defeated chaos in a cozy restoration of the social norm. However, the gothic theme of isolation does echo throughout detective fiction with the loner detective, separated from society by a superior intellect and a strong sense of justice.

Crichton has produced four detective novels in four distinctly different styles, all of which have achieved popularity. The whodunit *A Case of Need*, which he published under the name Jeffrey Hudson, won the Mystery Writers of America Edgar Award for best novel in 1968. Here, circumstances force a doctor into amateur detection to save a friend who has been falsely accused of murder. In 1979 Crichton won another Edgar for *The Great Train Robbery*, a fact-based novel set in Victorian England. This crime novel focuses on the criminal and how he successfully outwits police at every turn. In 1992 Crichton's police procedural, *Rising Sun*, showed professional police officers engaged in a case. Most recent is his 1994 novel of detection, *Disclosure*, where the victim of the crime and the readers know the identity of the true criminal, but the victim must engage in amateur investigation in order to clear his own name and prove the culprit's guilt. In all of these novels, good ultimately triumphs, though not without suffering lasting wounds in its battle for justice. Each of the investigating heroes finds himself isolated from the rest of society because of his refusal to conform to traditional conventions and his dedication to a personal code of honor.

Adventure Fiction

Closely aligned with detective fiction is another important development in nineteenth-century popular literature: the adventure novel. Gothic and detective fiction, especially the immensely popular Sherlock Holmes stories, showed readers that contemporary society and science could be very exciting (Stevenson, 100–101). Stylistically, adventure novels developed a clean, journalistic presentation that read like nonfiction. Authors set their stories in exotic locales, created suspense, and held it through the development of short chapters and frequent climaxes. Two types of adventure novels are of particular importance in the development of Michael Crichton's work: those that focused on lost worlds, and the type of novel known as the thriller.

In the nineteenth century, growing interest in archaeology and exploration contributed to the public interest in myths of fabulous ancient worlds lost to modern society. Perhaps the best known example of this is *King Solomon's Mines* (1885), by H. Rider Haggard. This travel tale about a lost city has never been out of print. Haggard drew on his own experiences in Africa. In this tale, the hero, Allen Quartermain, searches for the source of the ancient king's wealth. From Haggard's foundation grew the non-Holmes novels written by Arthur Conan Doyle, including *The White Company* (1891) and *The Lost World* (1912), and the successful Tarzan series by Edgar Rice Burroughs (begun in 1912). These adventure stories presented previously unknown worlds as the source of tremendous potential and fabulous adventure. They also emphasized that different cultures have a value of their own. In particular, they stressed the nobility and simplicity of the primitive lifestyle. Consequently, these authors felt pessimistic about the "advancement" of civilization and presented technology as potentially dangerous.

Crichton continues this tradition primarily in *Eaters of the Dead* and *Congo*. In both, the adventuring heroes travel to unknown lands—the desert of dread and the African jungle—on an adventurous mission, where they encounter completely foreign and extremely dangerous cultures. The wendol of *Eaters of the Dead* represent a lost race, primitive and vicious, who nevertheless possess the cunning to repeatedly attack and defeat more advanced civilizations. The guardian gorillas of *Congo* also threaten the heroes with their ferocity, but they represent an ancient civilization that had skills in animal breeding, communication, and training that modern day science clearly lacks. *Congo* relies heavily on *King Solomon's Mines* for many of its plot and thematic elements.

The second type of adventure novel important in Crichton's heritage, the thriller, represents a mix of adventure stories and detective fiction. The style of the thriller varies widely across an enormous number of authors and works, but its identifying characteristic often comes through thematic concerns. The thriller centers on a chaotic world in which a lone hero must battle the powers of evil to restore some element of justice. In this world, neither good nor evil is clearly identifiable. Consequently, the hero finds himself both hunting evil and hunted by it. Suspense centers on the hero's peril, which is usually resolved through coincidence or improbability. Nevertheless, the hero does conquer the villain who has hounded him and threatened destruction to civilized traditions and/or society, and justice is restored.

The many thrillers produced in the last two centuries have focused on a number of "ultimate evils." But none is more prominent (or provides stronger influence on Michael Crichton) than that of the "yellow peril," the fear that people from the "mysterious and seductively evil East" could overtake the "morally pure West." This concept of Asians as arch-rivals arose during the first era of European exploration in Asia. At that time, Europeans identified the East as a perfect society, peaceful and wealthy, evidenced by the "luxuries" such as silk and tea brought back to the West by the early tradesmen. Thus, Western jealousy of Asian economic superiority set the stage for the later yellow peril fear. When the West was less prosperous than the East, Europeans dreamt of claiming foreign riches for their own. Therefore, when the economic tables turned in the nineteenth and early twentieth centuries, it seemed certain that Asians would harbor a similar resentment. In the United States, fear of Asians gained momentum in reaction to the huge influx of Chinese railroad laborers. As early as 1880 P.W. Dooner's *Last Days of the Republic* depicted the conquering of the United States by the Chinese. Sax Rohmer's stories about the wicked Dr. Fu Manchu firmly established this stereotype in the 1920s. Asians were "described primarily by animal metaphors, depicted as being the predators of Western society." Throughout thriller fiction, Asian hunger for world power was "matched only by their hunger for the Anglo-American woman" (Hoppenstand, 280)—the primary symbol of white civilization. The "obsession with the yellow peril was deeply ingrained in the American imagination" throughout the twentieth century (Clareson, 17). This increased as Americans found themselves at war with Japan, Korea, and Vietnam. The stereotype of the evil Asian also revealed America's deep fear of losing economic power to these outsiders. This same economic jealousy has fueled the tensions between the United States and Japan in the late twentieth century as the East once again dominates economics, manufacturing, and trade.

While hints of this theme appear in several of his books, Crichton focuses on it in *Rising Sun*, where the plot centers on the economic crisis in Japanese-American relationships that began in the late 1980s. Crichton clearly depicts an Asian desire for world power and for white women, causing many critics to call this novel racist. Crichton also uses this theme in other novels. *A Case of Need* shows an Asian doctor who suffers racism of the yellow peril variety, and who is accused of murdering young white women through badly performed abortions. In *Congo* the team of heroes races against another team sponsored by a Japanese-European consortium to locate lost diamond mines. The discoverers of the diamonds will bring economic and military supremacy to their nations.

Science Fiction

All of these genres had tremendous influence on the simultaneously developing science fiction. Gothic brought emotional intensity and psychological depth, which early science fiction had lacked. It also introduced themes of the individual versus nature and a loss of true communication between individuals. Like detective fiction, science fiction emphasized the intrigues possible in our own world with intellectual and emotional involvement. Adventure fiction provided the concept that scientific advancement might be dangerous. Like adventure fiction, science fiction explored unfamiliar fantasy worlds and brought humans face to face with a completely alien culture. The results could be disastrous.

As a genre, science fiction has ancient roots in imaginary voyages. The greatest model is Homer's *Odyssey*, the ancient Greek epic of almost four thousand years ago. As early as 1638, Bishop John Wilkins wrote a book proposing that one day man would visit the moon and find a habitable world there. Fantasy tales like Jonathan Swift's *Gulliver's Travels* (1726) and Lewis Carroll's *Alice in Wonderland* (1865) helped keep travel literature alive as a fictional form of entertainment. Science fiction also drew from Utopian literature, which viewed scientific progress as the means by which humanity could achieve the perfect society. Authors such as the Greek philosopher Plato (429–347 B.C.) and Sir Thomas More (1478–1535) described such societies in their works. But it was not until the nineteenth century that science fiction began to solidify as an identifiable genre, primarily through the works of Jules Verne and H. G. Wells. In the twentieth century, authors such as Isaac Asimov, Robert Heinlein, Ursula K. Le Guin, Michael Crichton, and scores of others continually update and revitalize the genre.

Science fiction has continued to develop many of the same stylistic techniques used by other types of popular literature, revitalizing old fictional patterns. The detailed presentation of science appealed intellectually to readers. Jules Verne (1828–1905) was the first author who did not create an imagined technology. Instead, he used contemporary scientific knowledge as the basis for his situations. Verne's success set the stage for science fiction to focus on plot rather than character (a technique already employed with detective and adventure fiction). In his "scientific romances" such as *20,000 Leagues Under the Sea* (1869) and *Around the World in Eighty Days* (1873), Verne pioneered the "effort to explain every departure from the familiar and the known on a consistently logical basis. . . . His detailed adherence to or expansion of known scientific facts . . . never failed to produce a complete, and willing suspension of disbelief" (Moskowitz, 73–74). Another major figure, H. G. Wells (1866–1946), continued the same trend. Wells's background in biology and physics leant an air of truth to the scientific elements of his fiction. Wells's plots establish an "acute conflict, the sharper and the more irresolvable the better, and then [find] ways of overcoming the opposition without denying the validity of either side" (Huntington, 34). Both authors' novels succeed because they use contemporary settings and characters, and report in a journalistic style that fits contemporary demands for fiction.

All of Crichton's novels devote considerable space to the detailed depiction of science and technology appropriate to the time. Though *Eaters of the Dead* is set in the Middle Ages, it illustrates living conditions, weaponry, and modes of transportation in vivid detail. Similarly, *The Great Train Robbery* is set in late nineteenth-century England, and Crichton succeeds in making the time come alive for readers. His account blends mastery of contemporary slang, accurate historical research, and full understanding of trains, jails, and police techniques. His works set in the twentieth century benefit from Crichton's own medical and research training (much as Wells's background influenced his fiction). Crichton introduces readers to actual next-generation technological and medical techniques like computer-aided surgery and virtual reality, adding just a few fictional details of his own.

Because of the emphasis on accurate detail, science fiction is known for developing plot and setting rather than character. Perhaps the most unique element of science fiction is its attention to many aspects of human existence. Science fiction has remained concerned with reality beyond the psyche of an individual hero. It "focuses on problems that worry people today, often projected into the future and carried to their logical extremes" (Schwartz, 341). Clear examples of this occur in *The Andromeda Strain*, which focused on people's mistrust of the government in the late 1960s, *Jurassic Park*, which showed possible extreme effects of genetic engineering technologies, and *Disclosure*, which offered a disturbing picture of popular overreaction to politically correct issues.

The themes addressed in science fiction have remained remarkably consistent over the last century, despite the enormous changes in technology. First is the potential of technological advancement to improve our lives. Prior to the nineteenth century, society always viewed scientific development as the means to future happiness. "Such a view envisioned the perfectibility of humanity and state, creating an optimism that remains even today at the heart of much science fiction" (Clareson, 9). However, controlling this impressive technology is a humankind that is flawed. Verne's works focus on the "realization of the dangers involved in a powerful technology given to a not-quite-perfect man" (L. Rose and S. Rose, 17). Wells presented man's use of technology as destructive. Faced with the horrors of the American Civil War and the problems resulting from the Industrial Revolution, the public began to believe that "technology" could be dangerous. In addition, people feared that the theory of human evolution might not imply continued *improvement* of the species, but merely continuous *change*. It might allow humans to devolve into beasts. In *The Island of Dr. Moreau* (1896) Wells explored this fear, and the lines between man and beast begin to blur. The novel shows, in Philmus's words, "the prophetic myth of man's partial animality as an irrational creature motivated by fear and desire" (Clareson, 27). This early vision of genetic engineering suggests that human traits and animal traits might be determined not by genetics but by behavior.

Crichton picks up this question about the nature of humanity in *The*

Terminal Man, Sphere, and *Jurassic Park,* all of which explore the natural order of the world and humanity's role in it. Crichton's scientists and explorers, like those in gothic and science fiction, continue to push the boundaries of their role, altering humans, animals, and the environment to suit the needs they have identified as important. As a result, they often meet with tragedy. Even *Eaters of the Dead* explores the nature of humanity by comparing the Norse with the wendol, who, Crichton suggests, represent an earlier evolutionary version of modern people.

When this technological and irrational human race encounters other beings, the result can be disastrous. Humans and their institutions all fail to act responsibly when faced with ethical issues. Science fiction forces readers to face humanity's inability to control its technology, and has made the international version of "keeping up with the Joneses" a horrifying reality. Now nations race for space, stockpile weapons, wage biological warfare, and destroy the earth's environment. The illusion of continuing progress is now widely seen as nothing more than fiction. Public trust in traditional institutions has deteriorated into suspicious discontent. As first suggested in Wells's *The War of the Worlds* (1898), concepts of civilization and humanity are relative. "The human-alien opposition generates a process of constant reinterpretation and reexamination of the bases of similarity and of difference. [In *The War of the Worlds*] . . . perhaps the Martians are not aliens at all but simply super-humans" (Huntington, 42).

Crichton later echoes these themes in most of his novels. Any group identified as "other" or separate from mainstream culture—from the actual aliens of *The Andromeda Strain* and *Sphere,* to the animals of *Congo* and *Jurassic Park,* to the Asians of *Rising Sun* and the powerful women of *Disclosure*—forces the heroes to reexamine themselves and their own limitations, and whether or not recent changes in technology and society have actually improved life.

In the twentieth century, a new reason for the faltering of humanity has arisen. As with the theme of the yellow peril in adventure fiction, science fiction also has become concerned with economics as the source of trouble. New visions of greed-driven scientists make technological "progress" even more suspicious. Now scientists work not for the satisfaction of scientific achievement, but for the financial rewards of producing marketable consumer goods. They do not consider the environment, human life, or morality. The Americans who once identified Asians as greedy and dangerous now express an antiscientific bias.

This clearly appears in much contemporary science fiction. Crichton, who had toyed with this theme in *The Andromeda Strain* and *The Terminal Man*, highlights it in *Jurassic Park*.

Throughout its history and into the twentieth century, popular literature seems to focus on the same central issue. Humans are incapable of fulfilling the potential of their intellect because of the blinding desires of pride and greed. Modern Western culture had made "a state religion of science and technology" (Ross, 532). Now, however, it finds that devotion inadequate for personal health, for a culture that will survive. Man's "self deification cannot obscure the irrationality hiding behind his reason nor the tendency of a run-away technology to make man the plaything of his own playthings" (Berger, 3–5). The failure to maintain an appropriate perspective on scientific work, in the context of moral and environmental issues, leads to catastrophe. Popular fiction now regularly addresses crises of exploitation: "the crisis of science and technologism; the crisis of 'nature'; and the crisis of materialist individualism" (Ross, 533). People wallow "in absurd and stultifying creature-comforts, not questioning their . . . cost in human creativity, vitality, and freedom. . . . And the obsession with power is virtually motiveless" (Berger, 116). Every novel by Michael Crichton illustrates these harmful effects of pride and greed.

CRICHTON'S DEVELOPMENT OF THE POPULAR HERITAGE

Though critics identify him primarily as a writer of "hard science fiction," Michael Crichton claims: "I hate science fiction. I never wanted to be called a science-fiction writer" (B. Rose, 226). Crichton's work does extend significantly beyond science fiction, adapting elements of many popular genres for contemporary audiences. In style and in theme, his works are clearly linked to the nineteenth- and twentieth-century literary heritage outlined above.

Crichton cheerfully admits his reliance on the traditions of popular fiction. When young, he wrote short stories mimicking the styles of Edgar Allan Poe and Ernest Hemingway (Chambers, 97). Many of his novels intentionally update classic fiction. *The Andromeda Strain* rewrites H. G. Wells's *The War of the Worlds*, and *The Terminal Man* updates Mary Shelley's *Frankenstein*. *Eaters of the Dead* views *Beowulf* from a new perspective, while *Congo* modernizes H. Rider Haggard's *King Solomon's*

Mines. Sphere draws heavily on Jules Verne's *20,000 Leagues Under the Sea*, and *Jurassic Park* revitalizes themes from Wells's *The Island of Dr. Moreau*. "All the books I've written play with preexisting literary forms," says Crichton. "The challenge is in revitalizing the old forms" (Chambers, 95). Crichton revitalizes them by writing in a clean, cinematic, suspenseful style. He also injects his plots with themes focused on contemporary American concerns, appealing to the fears and desires of popular audiences.

Crichton's style bears three distinct similarities to the popular genres of the last 150 years. First, he creates details that make his fiction seem real. Critics widely praise him for communicating technological detail to novice readers in an understandable fashion. His specifics enhance the story rather than bogging down the plot. He extensively researches whatever area he writes about. The footnotes, bibliographies, and nonfiction introductions or afterwords he provides educate as well as entertain. Crichton also fabricates documents to enliven his fiction. Memos, computer programs, brain wave charts, and classified government documents are "reproduced" prominently in *The Andromeda Strain* and throughout the other novels. "I like to make up something to *seem* real," he says (Chambers, 95). Because he creates such realism, his novels succeed in the popular marketplace.

A second successful stylistic technique Crichton adopted from his literary heritage is the use of a plot structure based on many short episodes. Acute conflict also hooks readers at the start and keeps them reading with eagerness. The highly emotional and fast-paced plot lines that worked in thrillers and melodramas keep Crichton's readers involved. His conflicts center on important contemporary issues, presenting both sides in larger than life detail. This, combined with the detail he bases on technological fact, propels readers from episode to episode in almost unbearable suspense.

This intense focus on plot contributes to a third characteristic Crichton's works have in common with historic science and adventure fiction: weak character development. Critics fault him for presenting stereotypical characters, giving more life to plot and technical details than to humans throughout his novels. Traditional science fiction has been referred to as a "home for invisible men and women. One is hard put to name half a dozen memorable characters in all the annals of the genre" (Sanders, 131). This is often true of Crichton's work. His readers remember the diseases, the computer implants, and the horrifying monsters in detail. But most cannot name even one of Crichton's major characters. Perhaps this forgettable characterization is not neglect, but a purposeful tactic designed to show how the issues in such fiction affect everyone. For instance, in *Jurassic Park* the problems of uncontrolled genetic engineering do not belong to Drs. Ellie Sattler and Alan Grant alone—they belong to the whole world. Thus, the names and personalities of those individuals recede as Crichton and his readers focus on issues of universal importance.

Crichton adheres even more strongly to the thematic traditions of gothic, adventure, thriller, melodramatic, and science fiction. Though critics argue about whether his outlook is optimistic, cautionary, pessimistic, or grim, it does seem constant. "Nothing changes. This is the sum of all the parts that constitute Michael Crichton's view of the world in general, and the impact of technology on that world in particular" (Sauter, 21). Humanity's flaws remain consistent. They limit our ability to communicate with one another effectively. This, in turn, limits the potential value of technological development. Ultimately, Crichton calls into question whether such technology serves as a positive or negative influence on our future.

In Crichton's fictional world, humanity has three fundamental and consistent flaws: irrationality, pride, and greed. The conflict between rational, ethical intellect and primitive natural instinct appears in the novels' plots as man versus some alien force. That force can be either the beast from beyond civilization or the beast lurking hidden within civilized people's hearts. As in gothic and science fiction, individual and instinctual desires often overcome rational principles, so that even representatives of those principles, like scientists, fail to uphold them. Many times in Crichton's fiction, the alien evil is actually human. The beast Crichton's heroes face turns out to be of human creation—a gothic-style physical manifestation of some instinctual or irrational element of humanity. We see this in *The Andromeda Strain*, *The Terminal Man*, *Congo*, *Sphere*, *Eaters of the Dead*, and *Jurassic Park*. In addition, *The Great Train Robbery*, *Rising Sun*, and *Disclosure* feature evil driven by motives our society admires.

Coupled with this potential instability, humanity's pride becomes ever more dangerous in Crichton's view. People, especially the representatives of traditional institutions like big business and science, continually attempt to control nature. When they overstep natural boundaries and play God, disaster strikes. The creation crushes humanity and nature once again reigns. This point is clearly made in *The Terminal Man* and *Jurassic Park*. People's prideful self-assurance that they know what is best, and their false sense of control even in the face of crisis, open the door to catastrophe.

Catastrophe also follows humans who succumb to greed. As in science fiction and thrillers that focus on the yellow peril, greed serves as the foundation for most evil action in Crichton's worlds. Prideful attempts to control nature also stem from a need for power. Control, power, and economic stability are all ways to produce the illusion that the universe itself will not change, that an individual need not fear change. This inability to accept natural change relates to the irrationality and pride mentioned above.

The flaws of irrationality, pride, and greed combine to make humans practically incapable of communicating with each other. The very meaning of "humanity" is no longer simply genetically defined, but based on behavior. For instance, a man with a computer implant in his brain seems more human than the doctors who conduct their experimental research on him in *The Terminal Man*. Repressed emotions unleash murderous monsters that represent a part of humanity more beast than human in *Sphere*. The observations of a naive Islamic messenger in *Eaters of the Dead* reveal Europeans as barbarous at best. The loss of humanity, drawn from gothic and science fiction, both frightens and fascinates readers.

These limitations of humanity in turn confine the possibilities of technology, because technology cannot perform beyond the abilities of its creator. For over a century, popular fiction has worried about humankind's moral ability to handle technological advancements. Because of people's prideful self-deification, technology tends to turn on its creators and destroy them. In Crichton's books—namely, *The Andromeda Strain*, *Sphere*, *Congo*, and *Jurassic Park*—this threat is never entirely removed. It exists, waiting in some secluded area to encounter the next group of trespassing humans. Because technology is ultimately defined by the limits of its human creators, advancement in this area is never automatically good. In the end, this suspicion of technology becomes a basic mistrust of all institutions, none of which are better than the humans who constitute them. They cannot escape the human limitations of irrationality, pride, and greed. So institutions cannot promise a better society until we better ourselves.

The ability to draw upon the rich heritage of popular fiction has helped Michael Crichton achieve his phenomenal popular success. His fiction creates exciting hybrids of traditional categories, utilizing the best elements of each. This mix stimulates even newer developments of the traditions within the framework of contemporary society. His books fo-

cus as much on contemporary social situations as on newfangled technology or on fictional traditions. Crichton's readers learn about their
contemporary world while being entertained with this vision of a strange
existence—one that proves not so strange, after all.

3

The Andromeda Strain
(1969)

Michael Crichton's first novel published under his own name, *The Andromeda Strain* (1969), rocketed to immediate popularity. It gripped millions of readers and inspired a successful film adaptation. It was even a featured selection of the Literary Guild. The success of this novel, written during Crichton's final year in medical school, helped him decide to pursue writing as a career. In turn, this eventually led him into directing film.

The Andromeda Strain tells the story of an American space experiment gone wrong. A satellite returning from a mission to outer space to gather bacteria for advanced biological weapons crashes in a small western town. Soon, its deadly microscopic payload kills everyone it contacts. The government eventually retrieves the satellite and isolates it in an underground laboratory. There, a crew of scientists races against time to discover a cure before a plague destroys the world's population.

This chapter looks at the development of plot, character, and theme in *The Andromeda Strain*. The techniques Crichton uses to create suspense are also examined. Crichton's use of the generic conventions of science and thriller fiction is discussed. Finally, a psychoanalytic interpretation of certain aspects of the novel is presented.

PLOT DEVELOPMENT

The plot of *The Andromeda Strain* develops through the presentation of multiple mysteries and the scientists' attempts to overcome conflicts and solve those mysteries. How does the unknown disease kill? What is the deadly agent? Where did it come from? How will it be controlled? And the question that seems to hold the key to it all: What does an old man with a bleeding ulcer, who eats a bottle of aspirin every day and drinks Sterno, have in common with an apparently healthy infant? The answers to these questions finally resolve the scientists' conflicts with the disease, with the government of the United States, and with time, which always seems to be running out.

The novel's primary conflict focuses on the struggle between humankind and the unknown disease. The arrival of the Andromeda Strain from outer space threatens all of humanity. It travels through the air and kills people almost instantaneously by clotting their blood. An entire town, Piedmont, Arizona, dies in only a matter of minutes after the local physician unknowingly releases the space bacteria. Investigators from NASA also die before they can even radio for help. When scientists return to the town protected by special sterile suits, they find the streets littered with bodies. Surprisingly, they also find two humans still alive— an infant boy and an old man. Scientists rush the infant, screaming with hunger, and the old man, suffering from a bleeding ulcer, back to their underground laboratory to search for a way to stop the disease.

In the lab, the scientists struggle to identify the characteristics of the deadly organism, aided by the most advanced technology. There it remains deadly, killing laboratory animals in milliseconds after exposure (141). Using robot-controlled microscopes and television monitors, the scientists eventually learn that they are dealing with a new life form (153), a crystalline structure which, unlike all life on earth, has no amino acids at all (221). Autopsies on the lab animals reveal that the disease solidifies five quarts of blood in just three seconds—a finding that amazes the scientists (166). It survives, they discover, by acting as a little reactor, changing energy to matter and the reverse. An atomic explosion would not kill the organism, but instead cause it to multiply with fantastic speed (240). Because of this, security becomes even more important, because the lab is equipped with an atomic bomb that will automatically detonate if any security breach occurs. This would not simply end the scientists' lives, but probably destroy the world.

The disease threatens anew when it begins to mutate into a new form. Initially this seems a more benign version of the organism, one that does not kill humans or animals. The new version is first reported by a military pilot, who, before crashing his airplane, reports that the plastic in his cockpit is dissolving before his eyes. Initially dismissed as the ravings of an insane disease victim, the guardsman's words later prove to be a factual account of the disease's mutation: instead of killing people, it now destroys plastics. This becomes just as threatening when it begins to dissolve the plastic seals in the security system at the Wildfire laboratory.

Another conflict the scientific team faces in its attempt to control the disease is the clash of their desires and those of the United States government. Fearful that the disease will spread before they can find a cure, the scientists initially beg the President of the United States to drop an atomic bomb on Piedmont, because they believe this will destroy the disease. The President hesitates, however, knowing that an atomic explosion would draw international attention. He hopes that the disaster can be contained and that no one outside the government will ever find out about it. While the President unknowingly saves the world through his inaction, he also allows the virus to spread.

Ultimately these conflicts are resolved when Mark Hall, a last-minute addition to the Wildfire team who has received little respect from the others, realizes the simple answer to controlling the disease. The growth of the Andromeda is controlled by pH levels in the blood, with minimum and maximum levels required for support. The range in which it lives is very narrow, Hall discovers. Thus the mystery of the baby boy and the old man is explained. The baby survived the disease because he cried uncontrollably during his exposure, which disrupted his breathing and made his blood contain too little acid to support the disease. The old man drank Sterno and hyperventilated from his ulcer pain, thus his blood was too acidic to support the organism (269). This information gives the scientists all they need to know to control the disease.

The final conflict the scientists face is against time. They do not have the luxuries of rest or recreation as they search for a cure. The strength of the virus and its ability to travel by air endanger the population of the entire world. With each passing hour, the disease travels further from Piedmont, closer to densely populated Las Vegas, Los Angeles, and other cities. Though they are safe in their underground laboratory, the scientists know that in order to save their families, their nation, and the world, they must work with superhuman speed and accuracy to find a cure. Even after they have found the way to control the disease, time works against them, for at that moment, a mutated form of the disease destroys the lab's safety seals and the atomic bomb is activated. The three minutes that Mark Hall spends attempting to stop the explosion that could destroy the world provide the most suspenseful moments of the novel. But that conflict, like all the others, ends happily for Crichton's scientists.

CHARACTER DEVELOPMENT

As is typical within the science fiction genre, characterization has little importance in *The Andromeda Strain*. Critics find Crichton's "lack of interest" in "the creation of people . . . amazing" (Shickel, *Andromeda*). That is why, in discussing the plot, references to the scientists as a group or a team are enough. However, that team does consist of four individuals. None of them are memorable characters, but Crichton has given them distinct backgrounds and personality traits.

The scientific team involved in the project called Wildfire is headed by Jeremy Stone. This biologist had won the Nobel Prize for biology work he did in his spare time while attending law school (37). He is young, brilliant, and fascinated by a wide range of topics. He can talk about scientific data, dirty jokes, and the dangers of space aliens with equal sincerity. These abilities make him willing and able to develop the Wildfire program for the federal government. Wildfire is an emergency facility for containing and examining any alien life that arrives on earth. Stone has no prejudices about the things worthy of his investigation. Instead, he devotes himself to understanding as much about the world around him as possible (283).

Joining Stone on the Wildfire team is microbiologist Peter Leavitt. He fits the team perfectly because he differs from the tireless, inquisitive Stone. A true pessimist, Leavitt sees the worst possibilities in any situation. He reminds the others of the care they must take in their work. At the same time, however, his imagination and willingness to take risks help the team proceed. His devotion to his work leads Leavitt to keep a nearly fatal secret from his colleagues. He does not tell the others that he suffers from epilepsy. Flashing lights, like the ones that indicate an emergency in the Wildfire lab, cause terrible seizures. Smaller seizures, during which Leavitt loses his memory for five or ten minutes, occur more frequently. Though not physically dangerous, these small seizures cause him to forget the imaginative theories he develops about Andromeda (200). This sets the team's work back even farther.

Charles Burton, the Wildfire pathologist, is perhaps the least developed character among the scientists. What he does is far more important than who he is. When he autopsies the lab animals who have died from Andromeda, he makes crucial mistakes that mask the truth about the alien organism (167). Later, when he does "discover" the answer, he doesn't realize it (236). However, his terrified reaction to his own accidental exposure gives the other scientists the information they need to discover ways to control the disease (256).

Surgeon Mark Hall joins the Wildfire team against Stone's wishes. Stone does not know Hall as well as he does the other men, and hesitates to involve him. The government, however, insists that an unmarried male join the team, and Mark Hall is their compromise (49). The government's Odd Man hypothesis indicates that single males make more appropriate life and death decisions than married males (105). The government needs such a man because the lab is designed to self-destruct in case of any security breach. An atomic bomb is automatically armed to destroy the lab and everything in it after a three-minute delay. During that three minutes, however, someone could stop the explosion—and the Odd Man hypothesis indicates that only a man with no wife or children can be trusted to make such a decision. So Hall—the only single male on the team—will carry the key that can turn off the atomic bomb in the lab. Though initially brought to the team as a compromise, Hall becomes the clear hero of the story. His intellectual strength helps him turn his observations of the Andromeda survivors into a cure for the disease (261, 265). Similarly, his physical strength enables him to turn off the lab's atomic device when it is accidentally triggered (278).

Perhaps the most memorable character in *The Andromeda Strain* is not a member of the scientific team at all, but Peter Jackson, the old man who survives the initial attack of Andromeda in Piedmont, Arizona. Jackson is a cranky sixty-nine-year-old who doesn't trust doctors to cure his bleeding ulcer. For two years, he tells scientists, he has treated his own pain by eating a bottle of aspirin each day. He has also been drinking Sterno. He does not seem to care that this makes his bleeding worse, and could blind him. "Well, hell, it made me feel better, so I took it" (177). In the ultra-sophisticated technological world of the Wildfire lab, Jackson continually voices skepticism about doctors, scientists, and the government. His ideas contrast with those the scientific team takes for granted, providing a broader perspective for readers.

THEMATIC ISSUES

The skeptical attitude voiced by Jackson, combined with the scientists' conflict with the United States government, suggests a theme important to all of Crichton's readers. The conflict between the government's agenda and the well-being of Americans focuses on the danger people are in. The President delays dropping the bomb because he hopes to hide the news of the Andromeda Strain from the public. A leak of that information would bring an investigation into the origins of the disease, which has been captured by an American satellite sent secretly into space to collect bacteria and bring them back to earth. These bacteria were to be used to develop new, lethal weapons. The project has remained top secret from the start, for fear that American citizens would stop it. Clearly the President does not want the public to find out he has engaged in the development of biological weapons, especially without their knowledge or consent, so he risks spreading a disease to save his own reputation. Only amazingly good luck in weather patterns and the speed of the virus's mutation prevent that disaster from occurring.

Crichton's picture of a government that acts secretly and dangerously rose from contemporary history. *The Andromeda Strain* was published in 1969, a time of widespread disenchantment with traditional institutions in America. The Cuban missile crisis, the Bay of Pigs disaster, growing tensions in Vietnam, and the development of tranquilizers and birth control pills filled the news in the 1960s. They all contributed to the American people's growing concern with established institutions like government and science. Even as recently as 1994, evidence appeared that justified these old fears. News reports revealed that government troops, and even some civilians, had been used in radiation experiments without their knowledge. As Crichton writes in *The Andromeda Strain*: "Few Americans . . . were aware of the magnitude of U.S. research into chemical and biological warfare. The total government expenditure in CBW exceeded half a billion dollars a year. Much of this was distributed to academic centers . . . where studies of weapons systems were contracted under vague terms" (45). Crichton's story suggests that Americans cannot trust the government, or the scientific community, to make judgments in the best interests of the average citizen. This theme is repeated in *The Terminal Man* and *Jurassic Park*.

THE CREATION OF SUSPENSE

Both the cast of characters and the details of plot bring mystery and terror to the reader. However, the creation of suspense in *The Andromeda Strain* is essential to the book's success. Crichton employs several techniques to make the novel more believable and frightening, including the use of verisimilitude, the setting of a ticking clock, and the creation of dramatic irony.

Crichton effectively creates verisimilitude—detailed descriptions that make the events of the novel seem undeniably real. This realism helps grab readers' interest. Reviews that call this a "non-fiction novel . . . believable, and seemingly informative" (Shickel, *Andromeda*) prove its success. Crichton achieves this by formatting the book as a scientific document. It opens with a file cover page (complete with top secret warning). From there, it proceeds to a lengthy acknowledgment section listing many military and scientific personnel who helped the author tell the story "accurately and in detail" (xi). Finally, it closes with a reference bibliography of over sixty-five items. Throughout the novel, government communications, laboratory analyses, top secret documents, and computer graphics are reproduced. In addition, detailed explanations of sterilization procedures, transcribed interactions between characters and computers, and lengthy descriptions of scientific tests carried out by state-of-the-art robotics create a clear and stunning visual image of the events in the reader's mind.

Crichton also sets the clock ticking to create suspense, orchestrating a situation in which the passage of time brings ever increasing danger. Then he constantly reminds us about the time. This is intended to make readers nervous. The opening of the novel makes clear the importance of speed as the scientists disappear from dinner parties and surgeries without even changing their clothes. Similarly, Crichton uses the ticking clock in the book's climax, when the computer automatically arms the lab's atomic bomb. Doctor Mark Hall has only three minutes to disarm it. As time runs out, Crichton invokes a novelistic equivalent of slow motion in film. He presents the scene from Hall's point of view by continually monitoring the computer's countdown. At the same time curare gas and darts, designed to stop escaping lab animals, gradually poison Hall, making him heavy and slow and disrupting his vision. "Time was passing swiftly. He could not understand it; everything was so fast, and he was so slow. The handle. He closed his fingers around it, as if in a dream. He turned the handle" (277). Crichton's technique grips readers while frustrating them by skillfully depicting a drugged state in a desperate man. We read on, breathless.

Crichton also creates suspense through dramatic irony, a narrative situation in which readers know more than the characters do. Therefore, readers recognize the misjudgments and errors the characters make. The scientists, convinced that the surface exposure to the disease has been eliminated by the atomic detonation they requested, do not rush their analysis of the organism at first. However, the readers know that the President did not drop the bomb and that the disease still threatens people. Thus, when the men agree to slow their pace (204), the reader wants to scream the truth loud enough for the fictional scientists to hear. In a similar way, readers know about the crash of the Phantom jet and the insanity of a highway patrolman much earlier than the scientists do. Crichton alerts readers to computer malfunctions and to scientists making incorrect decisions that will lead to terrible results. "What they did not anticipate was the magnitude, the staggering dimensions of their error. They did not expect that their ultimate error would be a compound of a dozen small clues that were missed, a handful of crucial facts that were dismissed. The team had a blind spot" (237). But thanks to passages like this, readers have no blind spots. They have a frightening awareness of how badly things are really going with this crucial operation.

GENERIC CONVENTIONS

Together with plot and character development and the building of suspense, Crichton employs the traditions of science fiction. He follows the developments made by other twentieth-century science fiction writers to bring his novel to a wide audience. First among these developments is the connection of science fiction to real technology and important cultural issues. "Science fiction, which once frightened because it seemed so far-out, now frightens because it seems so near" (Maddocks, 15). No longer do authors have to set their stories far into a future full of impossible technologies. The twentieth century has brought submarines, atomic weaponry, electron microscopes, satellites, and visits to the moon. As science fiction grows ever closer to the realities experienced by the general public, it becomes a more mainstream genre. People have begun to talk about "sci-non-fi," or science nonfiction, as fantasy "sneaked up on by the Facts" (Maddocks, 15).

Thematically, many sci-non-fi books follow the science fiction heritage, but their contemporary settings bring them new attention. Michael Crichton admits that *The Andromeda Strain* is a reworking of *The War of the Worlds*, a novel about the invasion of earth by Martians. Wells's work, and Orson Welles's classic radio version of that novel, sparked plenty of concern in their time. But they seemed hopelessly simplistic to the newly sophisticated space age of the 1960s. Crichton's aliens, however, are microscopic bacteria. To fight them, scientists must use the most sophisticated robots, diagnostic computers, and security systems. Thus the novel had a greater impact on its readers. They considered the novel a theory about "the most likely way experiments in germ warfare might turn against experimenters" (Maddocks, 15).

Crichton reshaped many elements that originated in science fiction (as described in Chapter 2) to fit the contemporary world. Most obviously, *The Andromeda Strain* is a variation of the man versus space monster tale, exemplified by Wells's novels and by films like *The Blob* and *Invasion of the Body Snatchers*. But it also deals with the theme of the man-made monster. The Andromeda invasion occurs because humans send out probes to bring alien bacteria back to earth for use as weaponry. Fears of a disease from space were very real in the 1960s, when spacecraft and astronauts underwent lengthy quarantines. In a sense, then, the Strain is a terrible creature created by humanity's careless use of technology, like Frankenstein's monster or the dreadful Mr. Hyde.

In this sense, *The Andromeda Strain* resembles Crichton's later bestseller, *Jurassic Park*. Both novels depict science growing so fast that humans cannot control it. Both illustrate a remarkable lack of vision—and in some cases, downright stupidity—on the part of supposedly brilliant scientists. Crises that result from the uncontrolled experimentation could have been prevented but, given the scientists' state of mind, were inevitable and thus predictable.

In shifting its form to fit the contemporary audience, science fiction also began to become more like the traditional thriller. Best-sellers in the late 1980s included a type of novel called the techno-thriller (the novels of Tom Clancy are a popular example). But that style of fiction was invented, many people say, by Michael Crichton in *The Andromeda Strain*. One critic praised *The Andromeda Strain* for being "narrated with the cool aplomb characteristic of recent spy stories (with memos and schedules and chains of command)" (Alloway, 571). This mixing of the two genres helped science fiction like *The Andromeda Strain* achieve mainstream success.

A PSYCHOANALYTIC CRITICAL READING OF *THE ANDROMEDA STRAIN*

Another way of looking at *The Andromeda Strain* that helps explain its continuing popularity involves psychoanalytic criticism. Probably no other breakthrough in thought has influenced the twentieth century as much as Sigmund Freud's development of psychoanalysis in the early 1900s. In addition to influencing psychologists, his theories of the personality have affected the development of twentieth-century literature. Though more sophisticated psychological theory has replaced much of Freud's work, his influence continues. As Ross Murfin asserts, "We are all Freudians, really, whether or not we have read a single work by the famous Austrian psychoanalyst" ("Psychoanalytic," 236). Freud's concepts of the conscious and unconscious; of the id, ego, and superego; and of defense mechanisms such as repression are familiar to all of us.

Understanding psychoanalytic criticism requires an understanding of the basic premises of Freudian theory. These consist largely of Freud's model of the human mind and personality and how they function. Freud envisioned the mind and the personality as two distinct organizations. The mind is divided into two parts: the conscious and the unconscious. Freud says that the normal human mind is *mostly* unconscious, and within that unknowable unconscious live the forces that motivate nearly all human action. His theory that the conscious part of the human personality represents only a small fraction of the individual rocked social and intellectual circles in the late 1800s. It threw into question a person's ability to know him- or herself.

Over this unconscious/conscious foundation of the mind, Freud places an organizational scheme of the personality. This divides the human personality into three parts, defined by their function in human life. The first part, the id, seeks pleasure no matter what the cost to itself or others. The second part, the ego, develops in both the conscious and unconscious through social interactions and follows the reality principle. It knows that to survive one must cooperate at a social level and not pursue only pleasure. Finally, the superego exists, like the ego, in both the conscious and the unconscious mind. However, it is not part of the self-image "I." Most often the superego echoes parental and institutional (church, school, etc.) ideals that an individual adopted while growing up. The superego produces the moral, judgmental self commonly known as the conscience.

When other people's expectations begin to restrict an individual (and this happens almost from the moment of birth), the ego and superego begin to take shape. The id, or unrestricted emotions and desires, begins to fight against the demands other people put on it. The ego forms to control the demands of the id, and to interact more successfully with other people. The superego eventually develops to watch over the id and ego when parents or other authority figures are not around.

Sometimes the selfish desires or emotions of the id seem dangerous to the ego and superego. This is because the id may want something that conflicts with what a person's parents or society may allow. Since the ego and superego do not permit such conflict, they act to repress such feelings in the id. In other words, the material in the id is not permitted to become conscious. The unconscious mind swallows it, allowing the conscious mind to deny it ever existed.

Such repressed emotions, however, do not simply melt away once repressed. They continually resist the division between the conscious and the unconscious, gaining strength until they can re-emerge, even if only for a moment, and express themselves in some way. According to Freud, such repressed material provides the energy and motivation for almost all human action. In other words, the unconscious mind, not the conscious one, controls much of what humans do.

The return of repressed material to the conscious mind can take several shapes. If a person undergoes an experience that repeats an earlier experience, the repressed emotions may come barreling into the conscious mind. This explains the occasional inexplicable reaction everyone has to certain people or situations. You may take an instant dislike to someone for no valid reason. Something about that person has probably triggered an unconscious reaction. While the memory that motivates your dislike remains repressed, the emotion itself escapes and influences your current actions.

More commonly, repressed material finds its way into the consciousness through dreams, but only in a heavily disguised state. Freud argues that dreams often seem confusing because people do not want to understand them. This is because dreams represent the repressed things the ego and superego do not want to acknowledge. Interpreting the meaning behind dreams involves close attention to the images the dream presents and the language an individual uses to describe them.

This theory on the interpretation of dreams leads quite naturally to the interpretation of literature using Freudian ideas. In fact, Freud not only inaugurated the field of psychology, but he was also the first to apply his new ideas to literature. In his 1900 study, *Interpretation of Dreams*, Freud often pointed to literature as well as to case studies for examples of human behavior. In addition, he wrote essays on imagination, creativity, the artistic life, and poetry.

Freud's use of literature helped inspire the use of Freudian theory in literary criticism. Initially, psychoanalytic critics used Freudian theory to discover more about the author of a work. Like Freud analyzing a dream to uncover the truth about a patient, critics analyzed texts to discover hidden truths about authors. Eventually critics also began to focus on characters in the literary works as stand-ins for the author. By treating characters as real, critics really discuss the author, who is, in effect, the history and unconscious of all his characters.

The focus on character ultimately led psychoanalytic critics away from the author. Before the advent of Freudian theory, characters had appealed to readers because they represented some shared element of human experience. Readers generally cared very little about what characters revealed about the author. So psychoanalytic critics began to analyze readers, asking why certain characters and plot events appealed to them. They believed that certain works please because they appeal to readers' needs to fantasize about dangerous repressed issues. This is especially enlightening when looking at the work of an extremely popular author in a particular time, or at a work whose popularity has endured over several centuries. What about it appeals so strongly to its readers' repressions?

Although other critics have accused psychoanalytic critics of reductionism—using Freudian ideas without thoroughly understanding them—the technique is still widely used. Today, most critics acknowledge that a psychoanalytic critic who understands both the psychological theory and the literature can discover layers of meaning that might otherwise never surface. That is what we shall attempt to discover with a psychological look at *The Andromeda Strain*.

The central questions throughout the novel concern the nature of the invading bacteria. They suggest an alternate psychoanalytic reading that appeals to a broader sense of human experience. In *The Andromeda Strain*, Crichton shows us a familiar world, but full of alien things that threaten humanity. Similarly, each of us encounters "aliens" every day in the other people with whom we must successfully interact if we hope to survive. Although Freud did very little work with the interactions between people, psychologists who followed him did. Object relations theory suggests that interactions with others help form the individual's self-concept. In object relations theory, environment influences the way an individual develops. This idea, combined with the basic Freudian personality structure from which it grew, provides an interesting reading of *The Andromeda Strain*.

As individuals, each of us continually sends parts of ourselves out into the strange world populated by other people. The clothes we wear, the language we use, our facial expressions, the emotions we display all go out into the world beyond us. We try to do things that will help us survive. Successful connections in that world affirm that what we have done is right. That encourages us to continue to grow. Unsuccessful interactions cause us to reevaluate our plans. If someone expresses an opinion, and others laugh at him, he reacts. His defenses may attempt to ignore the pain of that laughter by insisting that "they don't understand." But once that threat is under control, he will try to understand why the others laughed. That way, the same error cannot happen again. From there he will search for a more profitable way to interact with others.

The Andromeda Strain parallels this fundamental human situation. As humans we reach beyond ourselves, hoping for interactions that will bring us success and reaffirm our power. The search for the strongest biochemical weapons is much like each individual's urge for security. The nation acts, on a grand scale, just like the single person who wants control and safety. That does not mean that every person is power-hungry. Every nation does not desire to become a dictatorial state. However, power is necessary to gain control, which in turn leads to security, something all humans desire.

The search for power and security can be dangerous. It involves taking risks. We must send parts of ourselves into the world beyond us and wait to see whether or not they return. If they do come back, we must deal with the outside world's response. Most of us have at some time, in a class or a meeting, tossed out a controversial, original point of view and waited, sometimes holding our breath, to see how others will react. That is the same sort of action humanity takes in *The Andromeda Strain*. It sends probes into outer space and waits to see how the universe will react.

The Freudian twist to all this is, of course, the unconscious. We all know that the unconscious exists, but we cannot control it. Therefore, it often does things without our conscious knowledge. Unconscious power often seems to work both for us and against us. In Crichton's novel, the federal government, like the unconscious, acts in secret, uncontrollable, and potentially dangerous ways. It sends "messages" or probes out to the world beyond without the knowledge or consent of the public—including the scientists who have advised the government. These probes, in turn, gain a response from space that creates a threatening situation.

Once people perceive the threat, they respond in several ways. First they act defensively, ensuring that the unwelcome response from the outer world is contained. Individuals may lash out in anger, or simply withdraw to create a smaller target for any further hostility. Later, when the situation seems contained, the individual can examine the situation and begin to learn from it. What was the nature of the other's response? What action of ours led to it? Or was it caused by some incomprehensible motivation? How can we keep it from happening again? The Freudian superego plays a large part in this analysis, providing a moral sounding board against which an individual can judge his or her actions. Often, as in *The Andromeda Strain*, the fault is placed on the self. It is the individual—in this case, humanity—who has brought disaster upon itself by unwise action. In the novel, the scientists initially admit that the most likely source of the deadly organism is a contaminated spacecraft. Yet such guilt is unpleasant. Therefore, people try to deny any association with fault. We conveniently forget certain facts as we cleanse ourselves of responsibility. The typical pattern appears in the actions of the Wildfire crew, who, having acknowledged earth as the most likely source of the Andromeda organism (126), ultimately term it "entirely alien" (217). Humanity, then, escapes blame for this disaster. Only the outer world carries fault, and the individual retains the illusion of being intact and secure.

These issues, so familiar to each of us on a personal as well as a social scale, help create the enduring fascination of Crichton's novel, which has lasted over twenty-five years. The novel seems to strike a nerve with audiences across the decades. One recent critic found it powerful as "an eerie precursor of the AIDS epidemic" (Goldner, 4). Stephen King's blockbuster novel *The Stand* and the highly rated television mini-series based on it owe much to Crichton's earlier work. Americans continue to feel suspicious of government and scientific activities. And the psychological theme compels us. As individuals we must understand ourselves and the world around us to achieve security and survival. But although, like the scientists in *The Andromeda Strain*, Crichton's audiences may come to understand a great deal about themselves and the world around them, they can never achieve complete control. Too many powerful, unpredictable events continually affect existence. Though people try their best to achieve their goals successfully, in the end, with each of us, as with Andromeda, it is "out of our hands" (285). That is the situation that perplexes humans throughout their lives and renders Crichton's narrative so appealing.

4

The Terminal Man
(1972)

Crichton's second novel under his own name, *The Terminal Man*, appeared in 1972 and continued the enormous popularity of *The Andromeda Strain*. At that time, critics raved about the book; one called it "one of the season's best" (Coyne, 700). It was "quite terrifying in its suspense and implication" (Weeks, "Terminal," 108). However, critics twenty years later generally judge the book only adequate. *The Terminal Man* allows readers to glimpse five days in the lives of Harold Benson and the doctors who have implanted electrodes in his brain to fight off his violent seizures. The mixture of man with machine goes horribly awry, and Crichton delivers another shocking story of the dangers of uncontrolled technological development.

This chapter looks at four aspects of *The Terminal Man*: how the conventions of science fiction affect plot development; character development; how plot and character communicate the central theme of the novel; and ways in which the novel might interest a feminist critic.

PLOT DEVELOPMENT

Like *The Andromeda Strain*, *The Terminal Man* develops primarily from the heritage of classic science fiction. However, it adds the flavor of twentieth-century thrillers. This new style helped this essentially science fiction novel appeal to a larger audience. But the plot pattern stems almost directly from classic science fiction.

The story line of *The Terminal Man* draws heavily on the traditions begun by Mary Shelley in *Frankenstein* and continued by H. G. Wells in *The Island of Dr. Moreau*. All these novels focus on the conflict of man against nature. Here the human scientists struggle against the mysteries of life. They want to learn how to create life and use their knowledge to build creatures better than humans. In *Frankenstein*, the mad doctor uses parts from dead bodies to piece together a creature of colossal strength. In *Island*, Wells's doctor combines man and beast. Ultimately, both succeed in creating a new, partially human creature.

The plot of *The Terminal Man* varies little from this classic pattern. A team of scientists in the Neuropsychiatric Research Unit (NPS) seeks to create smarter humans. To do this, they combine the human brain with miniaturized computers. Their first experiment on a human involves a man named Harold Benson, a mild-mannered computer operator who suffered a head injury in an auto accident. As a result, he experiences blackouts during which he attempts to murder people. To control his violence, the scientists connect Benson to a miniature computer. This should end his violent seizures by electronically stimulating the pleasure centers of his brain. Benson, who hates his own uncontrollable violence, has little choice but to undergo the procedure, which will make him part man, part machine.

However, as the classic science fiction pattern indicates, the scientists fail to control their new creation. The new creatures possess unexpected powers and powerful emotions. Like any creature, they want to assume lives of their own, and resent captivity. The conflict of individual versus individual now drives the plot as scientists struggle to keep their creations in check. They treat their creations not as modified human beings, but as animals, ignoring their emotional needs. Abused and misunderstood, the creatures become murderous. Soon the scientists come to hate the creatures they so lovingly created. The scientists, who presume too much and fail to limit their own powers, create only misery for themselves, their creatures, and the innocent people around them.

Like the lonely monster of *Frankenstein*, Harold Benson hates the scientists who have stolen his humanity and made him part machine. Initially his anger is contained by the mini-computer's stimulation of his brain's pleasure centers. Every time he has a murderous seizure, the computer stops it by inducing its opposite: complete calm and total pleasure. Soon, Benson's own impulses begin to override the power of the computer, and the scientists lose their control. Benson's brain quickly learns that to bring about more frequent pleasure stimulations it must have more frequent violent seizures. Soon Benson is having them almost continuously—a situation that will cause him to have a prolonged murderous seizure in only a matter of hours. When the scientists try to modify Benson's stimulations, they discover that he has disappeared from the hospital and is roaming Los Angeles freely.

Once free of the scientists' control, Benson sets out on a rampage of revenge. At first he attacks the people who merely happen to cross his path, murdering them with inhuman ferocity. The scientists and the police attempt to find him, but repeatedly fail. Then he turns his attention to his creators. His psychologist, Dr. Janet Ross, barely escapes death when he attacks her in her apartment. Only her knowledge that microwaves will disrupt his brain pacemaker and cause him unbearable pain saves her. Eventually, Benson sets out to hurt the scientists by destroying the thing they love most. In *The Terminal Man*, that loved object is the main computer at the hospital. Without it, none of the research work of the NPS can continue. By destroying the computer, Benson can gain revenge on the hated scientists and assure that they will not create another man-machine.

Another conflict common to such novels is that of the creating scientist versus other scientists. In *The Terminal Man*, the staff at NPS, headed by Dr. McPherson, seeks to combine computers with the human brain to make the most intelligent creature on earth (198). They are so anxious to succeed that they move forward with their experiments, even though Harold Benson is not really an ideal subject. In conflict with them is psychologist Janet Ross. It is this conflict that propels the book. Her experience, not the surgeons' or their creation's, becomes the central point of view in this novel. Her cautious, moderate stance on scientific procedures makes her the protagonist of the novel—the hero with whom readers sympathize. She believes that the experiments themselves are fine, but that they should not be performed on unsuitable humans simply to satisfy the doctors' personal desires. She embodies the moderation that is the theme of this novel, continually trying to do the right thing both for progress and for humanity. Ross recognizes Benson's extreme mental illness, or psychosis. As his psychiatrist, she tries to save him from the potential disaster of the operation. She opposes McPherson and the others, arguing that rushing into the operation with Benson will not really provide the knowledge they need to move toward their ultimate goal. The only result will be professional advancement for the scientists. They ignore her advice.

Eventually Ross finds herself forced into conflict with Benson as well. As the book reaches its climax, Benson breaks into the hospital that houses the NPS, intent on destroying its computer. Ross volunteers to take Captain Anders of the police department into the basement to the main computer terminals. Officers guarding every exit stand armed and tense. When Ross and Anders arrive they find that Benson has already smashed machinery, from candy machines to computer terminals, with an axe. Ross continues to hope that Benson can be captured alive and be disconnected from the computer that controls him. Soon Ross and Anders locate him in the central processing room, and after a brief gun fight, both men disappear in a chase. Left alone, Ross discovers Benson's gun in a pile of destroyed records; just as she picks it up, Benson reappears, intent on attacking her. Though she tries to save him, she must also save herself. In the final scene of the novel, Dr. Ross kills her own patient, a tragic end to the story of triumphant scientific creation.

CHARACTER DEVELOPMENT

Because these conflicts are based on the personalities of individuals, character development in *The Terminal Man* has an important effect on plot and theme. As noted in Chapter 2, characterization is not an important feature of science fiction. Instead it focuses on plot, scientific plausibility, and theme. The characters often seem stereotypical, based on general assumptions about age, gender, and profession. They rarely develop as individuals, but are figures used only to advance the exciting plot. Crichton's characters generally follow this tradition. They are more important for what they do or represent than for their individual personalities.

The three neurosurgeons, Drs. McPherson, Ellis, and Morris, represent the scientific establishment in three stages of development. All of them function in *The Terminal Man* as antagonists, characters who oppose the heroes or protagonists. They are the operatives in a secret quest for specialized scientific knowledge. McPherson runs the NPS unit, site of complex neurosurgery and experimental work, like Form Q. The future, he believes, will require a small computer with the capacity of a human brain. The only way to create it is to make computers from living nerve cells, which are tiny and operate on very little power. Ultimately, Mc-Pherson wants to transplant such a machine into a human being. He envisions all the glory as his when Benson's surgery—the first step in Form Q—is successful. When the escaped Benson commits his first murder, McPherson insists on keeping the truth from the police, potentially endangering more innocent people. When the information breaks, however, McPherson swiftly arranges to shift all the responsibility from himself to the chief surgeon, Ellis. As a result, Ellis loses his job and his home. McPherson is, through and through, an insensitive man who thinks little of anyone else except in their capacity to help him further his own project.

Dr. Ellis, though the senior surgeon in charge of Harold Benson's case, is really only a middle-level scientist. Therefore, he is easily disposable when trouble strikes. He recognizes his own weakness, so he tries to increase his power by increasing his fame. He hopes pioneering technical procedures like Benson's will help him. He is a man "determined to correct defects" (5), but his drive causes him to dehumanize his patients. Dining with the hospital public relations officer, Ellis thinks he looks like a rhesus monkey, and fantasizes about performing surgery on him (41). Ellis is not, however, as detached as he might seem. When a senior colleague questions his course of action, Ellis becomes emotional and defensive. He even resorts to childish displays of hatred, such as accentuating a limp and swearing (26–28). When Benson's escape destroys Ellis's chances for professional advancement, Ellis turns this anger on his own creation. Ellis's last words in the novel strike deep. Acknowledging that the disaster with Benson will destroy his career, this man who had devoted himself to fixing people admits, "I hope they kill him" (224).

Morris is the junior doctor on Benson's surgical team. He brims with expectation, power, and the romance of his professional duty. The glory and power of medicine enchant the fledgling doctor, who holds high hopes for rapid achievement. He admits that he joined NPS because of the opportunities it offered for fame and advancement (54). He craves control, competing with everyone for everything. Remarkably conceited, he loves his work because it makes him important to other people (7). When his pager goes off, he responds proudly (44). That sense of duty, however, ultimately leads to disaster for Morris. He is the only person in the novel clever enough to track down the escaped Benson. But his pride in his duty overcomes his cleverness and leads to injury. Knowing the savagery of Benson's seizures, Morris hides and prepares to defend himself from the oncoming maniac. When Benson pleads for help, though, Morris's pride in his position as doctor undoes him. "Benson was the patient and he was the doctor. . . . Benson would do as he was told. . . . as his doctor he had a duty to help him" (221). Too much importance placed on self and personal beliefs undoes the young scientist as completely as it destroys the others.

One scientist stands outside this research triumvirate, opposing them in more ways than one. *The Terminal Man* features only one fully developed character, Dr. Janet Ross. Crichton shows readers that Ross has strong views about experiments on human subjects. But she also has developed some anxiety about her relationships with men. Ross clearly grew to maturity, both physically and professionally, in worlds that honored only the masculine. Therefore, to achieve recognition and success, she had to adapt herself to that mold whether she wished to or not. Crichton tells us that as a female, she has felt like "an intruder all her life" (59). Her father really wanted a son who would follow in his footsteps and become a surgeon. Crichton implies that Ross herself entered medicine to fulfill her father's desires. Though she remembers her father as courtly (30), that adjective implies emotions never expressed. Her father never appreciated his daughter's professional achievements, and even missed her medical school graduation ceremonies because of a sudden illness (257).

This sense of being treated as a female first and as a person second continues in Ross's adult life. Her colleagues clearly would rather have a male psychiatrist in their hospital. She is annoyed when the men in the doctors' lounge change their behavior when she is present. "She didn't give a damn if they were raucous, and she resented being made to feel like an intruder" (59). Similarly, her boyfriend, Arthur, a wealthy playboy who flies her to Mexico City for taco dinners, values her only as a woman. Soon, however, it becomes clear to Ross that Arthur has no interest in her work or her achievements. She must face the fact that this man—like her father and colleagues—reacts to her primarily because of her gender, not because of her personality.

More important, Crichton's words reveal that Ross herself has traditional prejudices about men and women. She uses these to judge herself and to plan her future. She equates femininity with frivolity and silliness, and views her professional choice and her self as distinctly outside the feminine realm. Society has taught her what femininity requires, and she finds it inadequate, yet when she reaches for traditionally masculine goals, she feels insecure or guilty about her lost femininity. For instance, in surgery, when her sterile gloves tangle over her fingers, she immediately checks to see if the nurses and doctors around her saw the blunder. In addition, her assessment of her own looks reveals this guilt. Though her male colleagues consider her very good looking, "she often wished she were more softly feminine" (14). These thoughts indicate the extent to which Ross feels her actions are continually observed and harshly judged.

Nevertheless, Ross tirelessly urges kind treatment of others, even scientists. When the scientists ignore her advice about Benson, she remains committed to him as a human being. She is the only doctor who never loses sight of Benson's feelings and experience, as her reminder to the hospital staff indicates: "One should remember also that he is a highly intelligent and sensitive man. . . . His articulate manner may lead one to forget that his attitudes are not willful. . . . Beneath it all he is frightened and concerned about what is happening to him" (39–40). But when the press finds out about the experiment and threatens to stop it, she grows angry. They use emotionally charged rallying cries like "mind control," which stop the public from thinking rationally about the situation. She longs for clear information to reach a responsible public who can think critically about the issues at hand and help control the attitudes she fights within the scientific community. For it is these attitudes within the NPS research unit that create situations like Harold Benson's.

With the development of Benson's character Crichton makes his most significant departure from the science fiction heritage discussed above. In *Frankenstein*, the creature becomes one of two main characters, and, through the monster's own retelling, readers experience the torments of his life. In *The Terminal Man*, however, Benson the creature remains silent about and unconscious of his experience. This affects the development of readers' sympathy for and interest in Benson. In effect, Crichton lines up his readers with the novel's scientists. We are reminded, primarily through Janet Ross, that Benson is an innocent victim who suffered a head injury in a car accident, something that could happen to any of us. As Ross observes, "he was a good person, an honest and frightened person. Nothing that had happened was his fault" (260). This injury causes permanent ADL (a disinhibitory lesion) which brings on violent blackouts or seizures and causes Benson to grow mentally unstable when not blacked out. His mania has focused on machines, which he believes are conspiring to take over the world. Crichton makes him so crazed and paranoid that he functions more as a device to move the plot along than as a character. He provides episodic conflict—the actions that drive the novel from episode to episode—while the thematic interest lies in the interaction of the characters around him.

Completely separate from the workings of this scientific drama, but intimately affected by it, are the people of Los Angeles, represented in this novel by Captain Anders of the police department. This young professional is quite bright, challenging the scientists' low opinion of everyone not connected to medicine (171). Though he does have trouble accepting the violence of Benson's rages, he has no trouble understanding the implications of his attachment to a computer and an atomic power pack (239–240). He does not blame the scientists for the problem their experiments have produced, but he does expect their full cooperation in righting the situation. And from the start he establishes a comfortable, honest, give-and-take relationship with Janet Ross, thereby allying him with cautious responsibility. Anders represents Crichton's idealized public. He is interested in science and intelligent enough to understand it, sympathetic to the needs of responsible research, and effective in controlling the dangerous results of irresponsible work. This is the sort of person Crichton calls upon all of us to become.

THEMATIC ISSUES

Taken together, the major characters in *The Terminal Man* represent various perspectives in the greater social drama Crichton wants to explore. Here, scientists proceed on their own questionable agendas. Inhuman creatures are born of their scientific experiments. And the innocent public will suffer from these experiments unless they begin to communicate with the scientific community.

Crichton features contemporary technology in the novel to inspire readers to become more aware of what researchers are doing. *Time* magazine pointed out that "mind control through psychosurgery [is] hardly in the realm of science fiction" because an article on that procedure had appeared in its April 3, 1972 issue (Sheppard, 87). Crichton established this realism with details from contemporary science that create the illusion of reality in a work of fiction. Critics say he "maintains credibility with a fine array of documentary props, including a page of real brain X rays" (Sheppard, 87). Crichton also includes "copies" of police reports, computer readouts of Benson's electroencephalograph (EEG) tests, graphs indicating Benson's increasing psychosis, and other documents used by the scientists. Readers feel drawn into the reality of the story because, along with the scientists, they receive much of the vital information directly. This aspect of his book has been praised above all others. "Crichton proves himself capable of making the most esoteric material completely comprehensible to the layman, no small gift in any writer. Even more important, he can create and sustain that sort of suspense that forces us to suspend disbelief" (Coyne, 700).

Though his scientists create human tragedy, Crichton does not use *The Terminal Man* to claim that all scientific pursuits are dangerous. In his introduction, he clearly states his theme. Science itself is wonderful, but the lack of social control over scientific studies creates great dangers. Narrow-minded scientists pursue their special interest until tragedy strikes. In a 1968 nonfiction essay, Crichton wrote about this problem in real life. "Medicine has begun to impinge on moral questions which transcend the technical problems of catgut and clamps and ligature points. And, as medicine deals with more fundamental questions of life and death, it will need help, for it is a peculiarity of scientists in general that they are able to say what can be done, but are much less adept at determining what ought to be done" ("Heart Transplants," 34). In his novel, Crichton has psychologist Ross observe that "brave surgeons risked other people's lives, not their own" (224). Very often, their real motive is simply "the pleasure of doing something new to see how it works" (Edwards, 20).

The Terminal Man clearly shows the dangers that could develop if no one supervises scientists at work. Crichton, like most science fiction writers, stresses the clash of what science wants to do with what is good for humanity. "Without restraints, they fear, scientific evolution may so outstrip plodding human evolution as to diminish increasingly man's control of his life" (Berger, 7–8). This is clearly what Dr. McPherson desires as he develops his Form Q experiment, a powerful computer made of living nerve cells. He plans to transplant this structure into a human, creating "a man with two brains" (198). McPherson never indicates why such a two-brained human would be a valuable development. Instead, he only hopes to solve all the problems involved with this idea. He primarily wants to see if he can make it work.

Crichton believes that those in the nonscientific community can help guide developments by accepting responsibility and becoming more involved. They do not because they believe that "they live in a world that ... [runs] along a fixed pre-established course. ... That attitude represents a childish and dangerous denial of responsibility," says Crichton (xiii). People must become aware of and involved in scientific advances, demanding more control and accepting their responsibility for the future of our society. Crichton returns to this theme in *Jurassic Park*.

A FEMINIST READING OF *THE TERMINAL MAN*

A similar focus on the issues of control and responsibility could shape a feminist reading of *The Terminal Man*. In particular, feminist critics might look at Crichton's depiction of women in a professional world traditionally controlled by men. Before suggesting such a reading, however, the word "feminism" needs to be discussed. Everyone recognizes the term, but few can define it clearly. Therefore, it is perhaps the hardest of all literary theories to describe. Feminism investigates not only literature, but sociological, political, and economic ideas as well. In that way feminism is much like Marxism. It presents a "conflict model of society" (Selden, 135) and is *"always* political and *always* revisionist"* (Guerin et al., 185). It cannot help but be those things because it suggests one central alternative to tradition: equal possibilities for men and women in all areas of experience. Because of its revision of thought in so many areas, some critics claim that "feminism represents the single most important social, economic, and aesthetic revolution of modern times" (Guerin et al., 183).

Most critics agree that feminist agendas fall into three broad categories. The first is gynocriticism, or a concern with women as writers who focus on the female experience. Many gynocritics believe that women have a way of communicating distinct from men. They seek female writers as models for experience and expression. This branch of feminism has rediscovered many texts by women and has studied women's struggles to express their experiences in a male-dominated world. This aspect of feminism is, however, not applicable to a study of Michael Crichton, a male writer.

The second significant type of feminist criticism is "feminist critique" (Showalter, 1225), which examines women as readers of texts written by both men and women. It explores the way in which "the hypothesis of a female reader changes our apprehension of" characters, situations, and themes in texts (1225). This has provided new readings of classics that have traditionally been evaluated only by male critics. Many critics caution against the potential dangers of such reading, however, arguing that the social and historical context of a work is essential to understanding the author's choices. For instance, they believe a twentieth-century feminist critic cannot blame a medieval male writer for failing to portray women lawyers, because they simply did not exist in the eleventh century. When examining current works of literature, this aspect of feminism provides interesting debate. Through it, both male and female critics encounter and comment upon a novel at the same time, often with remarkably interesting results.

Both of these aspects of feminism have also been dubbed "gender studies" in recent years. They share the idea that gender difference determines a great deal about a person's life experience. Thus it also affects one's means of communicating, writing, or reading. A third school of thought, egalitarian feminism, does not believe this, however. While some argue that this third perspective has little to do with feminism, others insist that it is the core of feminist philosophy. This perspective is founded on the idea that males and females are more similar than different, and that critics should stress this sameness of experience and perspective among men and women. It argues that emphasizing difference has been used for centuries by men to exclude and oppress women. These critics argue that women will achieve equality only by denying any fundamental difference. Instead they must focus on the things shared by all humans of either gender. The dangers of reverse stereotyping—seeing men as always negative and women as always positive—are real if critics ignore the truth as shared by all individuals.

Recently, critic Annette Barnes has tried to identify the criteria that all types of feminists seem to accept. These include the beliefs that "women are not automatically or necessarily inferior to men, that role models for females and males in the current Western societies are inadequate, that equal rights for women are necessary, that it is unclear what by nature either men or women are" (9).

In addition, feminists question the value of objectivity when examining a literary work. For years, critics believed that the author's personal history and the social expectations of the author's time had no bearing on understanding literature. Literature existed complete in itself, to be judged by readers. Many feminists believe that such objectivity is both nonproductive and impossible. Instead, they promote subjectivity, or reactions based on experience and opinions, as a valid way to view literature. Feminists insist on recognizing that "the ways in which critics approach literary works, the questions they ask, and the answers they reach will all to some extent be determined by their beliefs" (Stevens and Stewart, 85). This, of course, holds true even for feminists themselves.

A look at Michael Crichton's presentation of women could reveal much about the ideas in his fiction. The interpretation of the text presented here represents a moderate egalitarian feminist view. In *The Terminal Man*, Crichton presents a clear picture of women as people who desire power and control, but who believe that only traditionally masculine behaviors can achieve it. However, their attempts to gain the desired status by mimicking men ultimately leave the women unhappy. The point behind these events remains unclear. Is Crichton implying that women fail if they merely adopt masculine characteristics? That instead they should construct their own model for success? Or is he implying that women are not capable of performing within a traditionally masculine realm? It is this issue that the following reading hopes to illuminate. Crichton's development of Janet Ross's character and the conflicts she encounters provides some insight into his assessment of how women pursue power, and what happens if they succeed. This theme is also developed in Crichton's later novel, *Congo*, which features a protagonist named Dr. Karen Ross.

As mentioned in the earlier section on character development, men seem to continually judge Janet Ross negatively because she is a woman. So the very feminine Ross seeks to become more masculine. This, she believes, will bring her the power and security to end her unease and her guilt. Her struggle for this power occurs primarily in her conflict with the other doctors over Harold Benson. By objecting to the scientific team's plans, Ross struggles to control them. Her opposition to the doctors is based on undisputed evidence of Benson's psychotic state. Only hours before the operation she continues to gather information that she hopes will influence the men. While they agree that conducting a behavior control experiment on a mentally ill patient will obviously yield less than desirable results, they decide to perform it anyway. This conflict, resolved by the men in their own favor against a woman who has all the rational evidence on her side, sets the stage for Dr. Ross's crisis concerning control during the rest of the novel.

The men's rejection of her opinion proves to Ross her obvious lack of power. This leads her through negative emotions of increasing severity— first anger, then depression, then a giving up of responsibility. Immediately after the surgery, she conducts a mysterious and juvenile display of rage in front of the doctors. She snaps at them, then storms out of the room, drawing curious glances from the men (79). This makes clear Ross's anger at her colleagues. But it also reflects the novel's attitudes about women's ability to communicate. Females can evidently only communicate in dramatic displays that draw attention but prohibit any sort of conflict resolution. Even when Morris attempts to ask what she wants, Ross cuts him off, thereby prolonging the unsatisfactory situation and further justifying her outrage. This game-playing is manipulative and dishonest, and though in reality people of both genders act this way, in this novel only a woman does.

Even after Benson's surgery, Ross hopes the men will honor her opinion and refuse to activate the implanted probes. When they do, however, her anger gives way to depression, which triggers some interesting fantasies. She imagines what life would have been like as a pediatrician. "Probably fun. Tickling babies and giving shots . . . not a bad way to live" (121). Having failed to gain influence in the masculine realm, she immediately launches herself mentally into the traditionally feminine role of caring for babies. Here her influence could be substantial because her gender would not hold her back.

When Benson escapes and the police launch a manhunt, control slips even further from Dr. Ross's grasp. Because she wants not to be right, but to be acknowledged and respected, she takes no joy in seeing her predictions come to pass (224). Eventually, she gives up her previous goals. "She didn't really care. She no longer maintained any illusions about her ability to affect the outcome of events. . . . she was in the grip of an inexorable process. . . . What would happen would happen" (242–243). The idealist who appeared at the start of the novel, gathering data, defending her patient's humanity, and trying to do the right thing, has disappeared. This connects to Crichton's theme in this book. Ross reaches the point of denying responsibility. She simply gives up and allows the consequences to wash over her.

The final confrontation with Benson brings Ross reeling back from her resignation to hopefulness, to fantasies of gaining power and establishing herself once and for all in her colleagues' eyes. With little warning she finds herself alone with the wounded Benson, pointing a gun at him. Faced with a deranged murderer, Ross imagines how this episode could bring her the respect of the men. She can save Benson's life, save Ellis's job and house, save McPherson's reputation and the NPS funding, and establish her worth in their eyes. "They would be grateful. They would recognize her achievement and appreciate what she—" (257). Their new respect would be so terrific, she thinks, that finally they would follow her recommendations, remove the computer mechanisms from Benson, and wait for a better subject. Finally she will achieve what she has wanted throughout this novel: influence on her male colleagues.

Ross's achievement of this confidence and status is instantly undercut.

She gains it only by using a traditionally masculine tool of power: a gun that belongs to Benson, a savage killer. She has picked it up out of curiosity, an interest in male symbols of power that she has expressed throughout the novel. Her attraction to Arthur's Ferrari (108, 121), her repeated descriptions of Morris as "cocky" (85), and her memory of a childhood boyfriend who had teased her with a snake (251) all highlight her fascination with male power. In the final scene, all alone, she finds one of the most powerful tools of all and picks it up. It was "much heavier than she expected. It felt big and greasy and cold in her hand. . . . it might tell her something about him" (255). To Ross, the gun clearly functions as a phallic symbol—a symbol of the penis—a representative of what is male, not female. Ross believes that maleness is power.

The final scene of *The Terminal Man* provides a complex finale to Ross's struggle for power and influence, and presents a bleak portrait of the possibilities for women. Ross wants to capture Benson alive, as much for her own satisfaction as his safety. But when he persists in attempting to get the gun from her, she fires, unintentionally killing him. When the police return to the area, the book ends. " 'You better leave this area,' the man said. Anders put his arm around her shoulders. She began to cry" (261). In many ways, this scene shows Ross in an admirable light. She accepts responsibility and acts sensibly, unlike all her male colleagues. She resists both her earlier inactive resignation (Ellis's state) and the appeal to her professional pride (which nearly got Morris killed). She desperately strives to preserve everyone's lives, even though she ultimately fails.

Crichton handles the violence deftly, clearly indicating that it is not an appropriate or satisfying means to power. A less sensitive author could have depicted Ross feeling justified in her homicide, satisfied in some way with the final acquisition of the power she has sought throughout the novel. But Crichton does not. He makes Ross almost ridiculously nonviolent throughout the novel. When Benson attacks her at home, she cannot find any weapon for self-defense (189–190). Later, when she leads Anders to the hospital computer area where Benson is hiding, she admits to never having fired a gun (246), a fact that clearly bothers Anders. When she faces Benson alone she thinks of the gun only as a means to safety for both of them: "She felt a moment of elation. . . . She was going to get him back alive" (256). Even when Benson attacks and she shoots him, she remains convinced that she merely forced him to dodge. When she does realize she has killed him, her fantasies collapse. Traditional masculine power does not bring the control she hoped for, but causes tragic destruction. While the gun does save her life, real control would have allowed her actually to rescue him. Instead, she kills her own patient, and with him, her desires. Her tears at the end may indicate sadness at these losses, but also a new awareness about the nature of power that may eventually help her overcome her dissatisfactions.

However, one might also interpret Crichton's depiction of Ross as full of shortcomings. Because she is not accustomed to having power, Ross cannot control it enough to use it effectively. She cannot even accurately fire the gun. The first time she pulls the trigger, the recoil knocks her into a wall. Because of this she cannot aim to disable Benson rather than kill him, which could have saved both her own and Benson's lives. It is through luck, not control, that she hits him at all with the second shot, saving her own life.

The men in the final scene indicate their understanding of her inability to handle appropriately the power she has achieved. On one level, the man warns Ross out of the radiation danger area and Anders comforts her after her trauma. But this scene implies another message. This woman needs to leave the area of masculine power because within it she endangers herself and others. Anders's gesture may be comforting, but it is also gender-specific; he would not comfort a male in this way. He reminds Ross subtly that she is, after all, a female, and will always be treated as one. It is at this gesture that Ross begins to cry, acting in a stereotypically female fashion, in her disappointment. The picture is bleak. While women can gain the traditionally masculine power they pursue, that attainment does not make them happy, because they cannot control the power. However, no alternative is proposed or explored.

The Terminal Man provides an important stepping-stone to the development of Crichton's later fiction by introducing two themes that run through later novels. Here, humanity's attempts to develop technology without careful consideration of the moral issues involved lead to crisis. Creations turn against creators with disastrous results. Crichton returns to this idea in *Sphere, Congo,* and *Jurassic Park.* In addition, *The Terminal Man* portrays women who seek or achieve power as makers of their own misery. As they piece themselves together from traditional gender roles, they experience internally the violence of dissatisfaction. This issue also receives further exploration in *Sphere, Congo,* and *Disclosure.*

5

The Great Train Robbery
(1975)

The Great Train Robbery proved a significant departure from all of Crichton's earlier work. It is the first Crichton novel that "did not concern itself with the impact of high technology on . . . society" ("Michael Crichton," *Current Biography*, 1993, 12). It is also the first that concentrates on characterization as much as plot. The plot develops through a fast-moving parade of episodes that grips readers and introduces thematic issues important to Crichton's readers. This combination produced a book critics have called an "exciting and very clever piece of fiction" (Weeks, "*Great Train Robbery*," 80) and a "wonderful crime-suspense-Victorian-cultural history" (Grumbach, 30). Crichton's mother has chosen this novel as her favorite (Goldner, 4).

This chapter highlights five aspects of *The Great Train Robbery*. The generic conventions of adventure fiction, not science fiction, shaped this novel. Those conventions, in turn, influence plot, character, and thematic development. Finally, an explanation of Marxist literary criticism suggests how a Marxist critic might read this novel.

GENERIC CONVENTIONS

Unlike Crichton's earlier novels, *The Great Train Robbery* is not science fiction. It is an adventure novel. As discussed in Chapter 2, the adventure novel rose to popularity in the mid- to late nineteenth century. It hinges on the adventures made possible by developing technologies. Such novels feature a clean, journalistic style that creates a nonfiction atmosphere. As in real life, good and evil are often difficult to identify. The heroes, however, continue to seek justice in their confusing world. To do this, they use their wits, solving problems with their minds instead of with violence.

Crichton incorporates all these characteristics into *The Great Train Robbery*, using the generic techniques developed in the mid-1800s. He sets the novel in that time as well. Crichton is, in fact, retelling the story of a real crime. He uses actual newspaper reports, court records, and historical references throughout his book. Exactly who is "good" and who is "bad" in these episodes remains as ambiguous now as it did over 100 years ago. The police officers—who should be the "good guys" of the book—continually appear as overconfident, lying bumblers. And the master criminal continually earns readers' respect and sympathy. Even generally conservative readers find themselves rooting for the criminal in this novel. Both the criminals and the police devote themselves to a patient game of wits. They avoid violence, instead manipulating each other through cleverness. However, the criminals clearly win this battle.

The Great Train Robbery also draws heavily on another, older tradition in fiction, that of the picaresque novel. Picaresque novels present a series of loosely connected adventures strung together in a story about one main character. This hero is a likable rascal who causes all kinds of trouble for the people around him. He generally starts life poor, undereducated, and with every circumstance against him. He survives, however, and even succeeds, through cleverness. He avoids honest, hard labor, because it leads to drudgery and stagnation. Picaresque novels often present a critical view of the established social classes and conventions that work against the enterprising hero. Classic examples of picaresque novels include *Don Quixote* by Miguel Cervantes and *Tom Jones* by Henry Fielding. Crichton's work has a more fully developed plot and cast of characters than the typical picaresque novel. His rascal hero, Pierce, succeeds by his wits. The novel also includes criticism of contemporary society.

Also adding to the nonfiction atmosphere of *The Great Train Robbery* is its depiction of the Victorian era in which it is set. Crichton's novel has been called "extraordinary because it is authentic" (Weeks, "*Great Train Robbery*," 80). Reading it provides a course in nineteenth-century history. Crichton's narrative not only details an actual 1855 robbery, termed at the time the Crime of the Century, but also includes mini-essays on many aspects of Victorian culture. Covered in the narrative are such topics as the development of the railroad and construction of terminals. Crichton explains contemporary theories about crime, the Crimean War, and London's population growth. He depicts several aspects of women's lives, and their roles in marriage, prostitution, and the law. He discusses animal-baiting, prisons, architecture, executions, and slums. That era's venereal disease treatments, white collar crime, and fear of premature burial fascinate modern readers. These examinations reveal an often surprising truth about the hypocrisy of the outwardly moralistic society of the 1800s.

PLOT DEVELOPMENT

The central conflict of this novel involves master criminal Edward Pierce and his confederates working against the Victorian establishment. Pierce wants to steal a shipment of gold from a fast-moving, well-secured train. In order to do this, however, he must survive many smaller conflicts. First, Pierce must recruit only the most skilled criminals for his team. He needs a screwsman, or safe-breaker, with nimble fingers. One of the four keys needed for the theft is kept in a well-guarded railway office. To break in, they must employ a snakesman, a small man who can climb walls and squeeze through tiny openings. The best snakesman, Clean Willy, must break out of prison before he can help Pierce. Then Willy and Agar, the screwsman, must break in, make a wax imprint of the key, and escape in only sixty-four seconds. Pierce and Agar then repeat the risky process for another key hidden in a darkened wine cellar. The first two main sections of the novel focus on these preparations.

While pursuing his goal, Pierce continually matches wits with some part of Victorian society. His first major obstacle is the rigid morality of the Victorians. Pierce must obtain keys to the safes that hold the gold. But two of the four keys belong to two highly moral upper-class gentlemen, Mr. Trent and Mr. Fowler, who pride themselves on being pillars of society. At first, Pierce can find no way to get their keys. So he investigates their lives, sure he will discover some moral weakness. Patient observation soon reveals the gentlemen's hypocrisy. The self-righteous Henry Fowler, the talkative banker whom Pierce plays for a fool, soundly condemns all criminal activity, but boasts of his own sexual exploits outside of his marriage. In fact, when he contracts venereal disease (87), he enjoys sex with a twelve-year-old virgin, in the belief that intercourse with a "fresh" will cure his disease. Instead, of course, he passes it on. Similarly, Edgar Trent, "the senior partner of a bank, a devout Christian, and a pillar of the respectable community [who] would never think to associate himself with members of the lower orders" (53), visits the slums to participate in rat-baiting, which is "flatly illegal" (54). These moral flaws give Pierce the footholds he needs to work his way into the men's confidence. This ultimately helps him copy their keys.

All of those difficulties are only preliminary, however, to the "Delays and Difficulties" that make up the third section of the novel. These are the obstacles caused by pure chance. New conflicts arise through the railroad itself. In preparing for his "flash pull," Pierce has bribed guards, memorized the train's route, and scouted out the station. But unforeseen events within the rail system continually present new obstacles for the master criminal to overcome. The gold shipments are delayed. Informants give Pierce the wrong dates. When the safes that hold the gold are overhauled, the robbers must be sure their painfully gotten keys still fit the locks. In the meantime, the police have accidentally discovered that Pierce is planning some kind of robbery, and have begun to follow him everywhere. Finally, an unrelated complaint forces the railway to increase security on the baggage car. Only hours before the robbery, the tightening of security on the train forces Pierce to match wits with his opponents. He must also outshine them in bravado as well by figuring out how to open the padlocked rail car door while the train is moving.

The hypocrisy of Victorian society does not always help Pierce, as it did with Trent and Fowler. Most notably, the hypocrisy of the police causes Pierce tremendous difficulty. These officers do not represent law and order trying to stop a criminal gang. Instead, they are lying thugs who intimidate suspects through falsified evidence and the promise of physical pain. Both Clean Willy and Agar give information against Pierce because the police fake evidence that will convict them on false charges. When Pierce himself is held as a suspect, the police submit him to months of "softening up" (251) in the most dreaded of English prisons. There he is forced to work a machine called a "cockchafer," a narrow box "where prisoners remained for fifteen-minute intervals, treading down a wheel of twenty-four steps." He also endures "the shot drill in which cannon balls are moved around a circle of prisoners" (252–253). He does not succumb to the police manipulations, unlike the others. His ability to stick to his goals enables him to overcome each obstacle.

In the fourth section of the book, Crichton describes the robbery itself in breathtaking detail. Here Pierce struggles against the best security contemporary technology can provide. Having overcome the boxcar security by passing Agar off as a dead man (Agar lies in a coffin with a dead cat to make the effect complete), Pierce must run across the top of the moving train from his first class seat to the baggage car in the rear. Once there, he lowers himself with a rope over the side of the speeding car, and while suspended, picks open the outside padlock. After Agar throws the gold from the train to a waiting accomplice, Pierce must relock the doors and return to his car. His struggles against the ripping wind nearly kill him, but he lands safely back in his carriage. Pierce's goal seems accomplished—but one section of the novel remains.

The final part of the novel focuses on Pierce's arrest and trial, probably the most difficult obstacle he must overcome to achieve his goal. While he has the money well hidden, he obviously cannot enjoy it from jail. His success depends on acquittal or escape. Crichton's depiction of the trial and the charmingly witty speeches Pierce makes there keep readers fascinated with this character who never gives up, even in the face of certain defeat. Pierce's ultimate triumph, when it finally comes, is well deserved indeed.

CHARACTER DEVELOPMENT

Adventure fiction usually focuses on the construction of intricate plots instead of on fully developed characters. *The Great Train Robbery*, however, features vibrant and lively characters in nontraditional presentations. In this crime novel, it is the criminal whom readers cheer on, and the police who engage in shameful behavior. This depiction of characters criticizes Victorian society and overturns standard assumptions about that age of repressive morality.

The central protagonist—the character who captures the readers' sympathy—is Edward Pierce. This delightfully roguish fellow brings readers' fantasies to life. Because Pierce is a criminal, he is not a traditional hero, but an anti-hero. He is a protagonist who does not have the usual qualities of a hero, but nonetheless possesses many admirable traits. Pierce is quite likable, "a most singular gentleman" (4), who is infectiously "exuberant in his approach to crime" (6). He is confident and knowledgeable in every circumstance he faces. He hobnobs comfortably with elite society and travels safely in the worst criminal slums. He deals honestly with his partners, and expects no less of them: "if you've turned nose on me, I'll put you in lavender" (152). When his partners inform

on him, he does as he promised, quickly. But most obstacles he overcomes with wit, not violence. He devotes months of patient socializing,
clever invention, and brave investigation to the attainment of his goal.
He never gives up, no matter how insurmountable the obstacles may
seem.

Unlike characters in the adventure novel, who exist merely to *endure*
the exciting circumstances, Pierce *acts* upon the situations presented to
him. He shapes events to suit his purposes. This power is one readers
wish they could have in their own lives. He overcomes treachery among
his comrades. He successfully eludes his conceited and bumbling opponents. He can adopt the dress, posture, and dialect of almost anyone.
His bravery astounds his friends as well as readers. When the police
prepare to arrest him, he coolly leads them on a wild goose chase. In the
novel's most thrilling scenes, he runs across the top of a speeding train.
Then he hangs over the edge and picks a padlock on the car door. Once
Agar tosses the gold out, Pierce must repeat the process in reverse. Only
this time, he runs against the wind. Pierce does not hesitate to risk his
life in order to achieve his goals. And, almost miraculously, he escapes
danger to reap the rewards of his efforts. In this novel, crime does indeed
pay.

Edward Pierce is the perfect criminal hero for a society that admires
independence and wealth. This is true of Victorian England and of modern America. Pierce freely admits that he pursues wealth simply because
"I wanted the money" (264). Audiences admire his commitment, his honesty, and his greed. "In a mercenary world this is perhaps the only motive that could humanize the dubious quality known as singleness of
mind" (Geduld, 65). Because he can admit his passion for money, Pierce
recognizes that most other people share the same desire. Others, though,
often hide that desire under moralistic speech. He "operates profitably
on the assumption that everyone is corruptible and no one is totally
trustworthy" (Geduld, 65) when offered the right price for their services.
Pierce becomes a hero because he embodies the common, but often hidden, desire to escape the confines of what society expects. He succeeds
as few of us can, with audacious action, gentlemanly conduct, and sharp
intelligence. Even after being captured and condemned, he escapes to
enjoy the money he "earned." That is the key to his success.

Standing in the way of Pierce are the novel's antagonists: the police.
They pursue Edward Pierce, or, as they know him, John Simms. In contrast to Pierce, Scotland Yard officers Harranby and Sharp are prideful,
dishonest, and violent. While Pierce clearly has confidence in his abilities

and takes pride in his work, he never allows his pride to become dangerous conceit. The policemen have too much pride in their own abilities, however. This makes them underestimate their adversaries (173). Their pride also makes them act outside of the law they are supposed to uphold. During their investigation, the police terrify, and even physically torture, suspects for information. Pierce suffers at their hands for nearly a year when arrested. He never receives arraignment or trial. Because he has not been convicted of anything, Pierce cannot legally be submitted to the tortures of the prisons. But he does have to follow prison rules. "If he broke the rule of silence ... one may presume that the guards frequently accused him of speaking, and he was treated to 'softening up' " (253). The police seem in many ways more criminal in their behavior than the thieves they pursue.

The main characters, and many of the minor characters as well, are depicted primarily through their specialized dialogue and daring actions. These details, interestingly enough, do not come entirely from Crichton's imagination, but from the newspaper, police, and court records surrounding the actual case. "Crichton is talented and canny. He makes no attempt to 'analyze' or 'understand' his characters. He gives us his ... [characters] straight, letting us listen to them talk in authentic street slang of the time, and educating us, incidentally, in the ways they live and make a living" (Grumbach, 30). Crichton's ability to use historical material gathered from government documents to make characters come alive is extraordinary.

THEMATIC ISSUES

The plot and character development of this novel both emphasize hypocrisy, thus suggesting Crichton's theme. Society, even an outwardly moralistic one like Victorian England, is riddled with hypocrisy at all levels, which destroys the chances for achieving any social ideals. Most notable, perhaps, is the importance of class distinctions in the dispensing of justice. Noble or wealthy people like Trent and Fowler believe themselves exempt from certain laws that interfere with their personal desires. In turn, the police support this by ignoring the upper class and their misbehavior. The police do this because they can exert little control over the rich. Instead, the police in *The Great Train Robbery* enjoy the thrill of enforcing their own power on the helpless far more than pursuing justice. The poor suffer from police terrorism whether guilty or not. This makes the police among the most despicable characters in Crichton's fiction.

Pierce points out this social inconsistency during his own trial. A mere robber of poor birth, he is treated far worse by British society than a nobleman who caused the deaths of hundreds of young men. Only months before Pierce's court appearance, Lord Cardigan led 500 men to their deaths in the famous charge of the Light Brigade. He led his men into a situation from which they could not escape in pursuit of honor and glory on the battlefield, and for this, British society calls him a brave hero. This same society, however, vilifies Pierce as a heinous criminal. With insight, Pierce pronounces, "I have killed no one . . . but had I killed five hundred Englishmen through my own rank stupidity I should be hanged immediately" (262). British society's honoring of law and tradition, regardless of the results they bring, indicates a lack of consistency which borders on the hypocritical. These examples and many more illustrate Crichton's theme of hypocrisy within this most moralistic and honor-bound of societies. His depiction of Victorian society fascinates readers through its unorthodox history lessons, and makes the essentially straightforward and intelligent Pierce seem even more heroic in comparison.

Pierce is the character who illustrates Crichton's alternative to the hypocrisy that riddles society. Pierce comes closest to escaping the restrictive standards of this society, doing what he pleases and saying what he thinks. Often these things are socially unacceptable, but they are the only route to personal freedom. He is the one person who enjoys the results of what he does. Instead of working for an inadequate salary, he does exactly what he wants and profits. Pierce's crime is almost an artistic self-expression. He takes tremendous pride in it. Even during his trial, he expressed great enthusiasm in his plot as he explained it to the court (261). The Victorian public and modern readers share this admiration with Pierce. Though a criminal, Pierce presents an attractive alternative to social hypocrisy. He is forthright, dedicated to his purpose, honest in his appraisal of himself, and as a result achieves happiness.

A MARXIST READING OF *THE GREAT TRAIN ROBBERY*

Marxist literary criticism is based on the works of Karl Marx. He is best known for *The Communist Manifesto*. Marxism interprets history as a process of social evolution in which all events and institutions are

based on economically motivated class struggle. Marxism condemns societies based on capitalism. Capitalism is the economic system in which
individuals pay wages to other people to work in their businesses. The
individual in control, who does little of the actual work, receives most
of the profits. Those who labor do so only for wages, usually inadequate.
This, Marx believed, prompted economic inequality. He envisioned a
different economic society in which profits would be equally shared
throughout society and poverty would be eliminated. This would happen when the workers in a capitalistic society became so frustrated that
they united in rebellion. This would finally establish a classless utopian
society. Thus, for Marxism, history becomes not a record of battles and
inventions, but an unending drama of classes competing for power.

Marx did not believe that work itself was negative. He viewed labor
as one way people expressed their creativity. He believed that humans
worked to express themselves. This, he felt, separated humans from animals. Marx defines humans as capable of "free, conscious activity"
(Fromm, 66). Labor of all kinds proves humanity's creative powers. All
humanity should enjoy the things created. Therefore, each individual
works for the improvement of him or her self and of society.

However, Marx believed that such equality never occurred in a capitalistic society. In capitalism, one class works to produce, while the other
class enjoys the products in exchange for wages. In this situation, work
becomes negative because workers do not enjoy the products they create.
For instance, the people who repair luxury automobiles do not earn
enough money ever to own one. The world created by the workers does
not belong to them. It belongs instead to the wealthy, who do nothing
to create what they own. Dominated by the upper classes, workers become dissatisfied with their lives. They begin to lose their humanity.
Because they do not use the products they create, workers ultimately
pursue only money. Their drives lose the human creative qualities.
Workers become fragmented and crippled human beings (Fromm, 68).

This particular reading of history views all art, including literature, as
embodying this unhappiness and the inevitable class conflict that results
from it. In the Marxist view, art is a symptom of social situations. It
expresses the point of view developing within the common people. It
helps the public express their fears and their hopes. Prominent Marxist
critic Leon Trotsky (1879–1940) wrote that art must be considered in
terms of the historical reasons for its creation. A Marxist reading of *The
Great Train Robbery* would therefore interpret the novel as a product of
the culture from which it sprang. However, because it is an account of

an actual event from 1855, it may be best to examine first how the actual robbery, which became known as the Crime of the Century, reflects the society from which it sprang. This, then, can lead to a discussion of why the story so captivates late twentieth-century audiences.

The Victorian society depicted by Crichton was without question based on capitalism. It also had very loose moral expectations for businesses. Fraud was not distinguished from clever business practice. Ruthless tactics were expected between competitors. Most white collar crime went unpunished (178–179). In Crichton's book, almost every character, poor or rich, is motivated by a desire for wealth. From the child informants of the slums to the upper-class manager of a London bank, everyone acts to gain more money. Pierce's theft of the gold, Clean Willy's betrayal, Fowler's social climbing, Trent's desire to marry off his elder daughter, Burgess's assistance to the burglars, and the police's use of informants are all prompted by the pursuit of more money.

While such attitudes are typical of a capitalistic society, they flourished in Victorian England, where financial success was linked to moral purity. This connection had two important effects on public opinion. If a wealthy man's financial status suffered, his colleagues and neighbors assumed him guilty of some wrongdoing. They then avoided him as a moral criminal. Thus the rich had to maintain financial success to preserve their reputations. At the same time, however, people assumed that a wealthy man stood in the highest moral order. They would dismiss his misbehavior as insignificant. "The higher an individual's standing within the community, the greater the reluctance" to call him a criminal (179). Therefore, conditions in Victorian society intensified the usual bad effects of capitalism.

As Marx suggested, this focus on the attainment of wealth for its own sake makes people very unhappy. At best they receive wages, which they must use to survive in an economy controlled by the rich. At worst, they become physically run down as well. In Crichton's novel, wealthy manufacturers regularly expose laborers to harmful conditions. For instance, as a child Robert Agar worked for a match manufacturer. "Phosphorous was known to be poisonous, but there were plenty of people eager to work at any job, even one that might cause a person's . . . jaw to rot off" (7). Rich men who contracted venereal disease could buy the privilege of intercourse with a virgin, usually a girl of twelve. They believed this would cure the disease (89). In pursuit of the high price this service brought, many young prostitutes had their " 'demure state' freshly renewed by the application of a small seamstress's stitch in a strategic place" (89). These workers are exploited not only spiritually but physically.

The maltreatment of one segment of a population by another drives ever wider wedges between them. In the nineteenth century, London neighborhoods became distinguished by the economic class—and therefore, it was assumed, the moral caliber—of their inhabitants. The slums were widely believed to be the origin of criminals (33). Movement between classes was difficult and discouraged by society. An upper-class person like Edgar Trent "would never think to associate himself with members of the lower orders. Quite the contrary: Mr. Trent devoted considerable time and energy to keeping those people in their proper place" (53). Similarly, an upper-class spinster could never take a job to support herself "lest she invade the rights of the working classes, who live by their labor" (59).

This severe class division, and the dedication of the upper classes to keeping the lower classes "in their place" led to the development of popular theories about crime. Victorians held the belief that technological progress meant that society was progressing morally as well. They also believed that poor social conditions were the sole cause of crime. When poverty disappeared, thanks to growth in manufacturing, they believed that crime would also. But as time passed, crime actually increased, as we see in *The Great Train Robbery*. Powerful social leaders remained dedicated to capitalism and ever-increasing wealth. This ultimately led to their loss of control over the poor. The lower classes, which continued to swell, wanted as much money as the rich, but they had no way to make such money honestly. Society had taught them that money was essential to morality and to happiness. So they would stop at nothing to gain it. Edward Pierce climbs into the upper classes through crime. But even then he does not stop seeking more wealth. He is the perfect example of someone seeking power through money. This terrifies the rich. They fear that such criminals will ultimately deprive them of the wealth they adore.

Later studies about crime have suggested other theories about criminal behavior:

- Crime is not a consequence of poverty, but a result of greed.

- Criminals are intelligent.

- Crime pays better than honest labor.

- Most crimes remain unpunished. (xvi)

Each of these suggests the important role capitalism plays in shaping crime in society. That crime is committed out of greed, not need, shows the power of capitalism's devotion to wealth. Intelligent people, with the capacity to understand morality, turn to crime because it is the most efficient way to gain wealth. Most criminals go unpunished, proving that society does not try very hard to catch them. This is because society has an ambiguous attitude toward crime, one that contradicts itself. On one hand, people hate crime. But on the other, they *admire* criminal daring and success.

The Great Train Robbery provides clear examples of such social ambiguity regarding crime. In the 1850s, the British expressed outraged shock at Edward Pierce's "heinous" crime. But they also admired it as masterfully plotted and audacious. Crowds gathered at the trial to see the criminal mastermind. Even Queen Victoria herself proclaimed him a *"most bold* and *dastardly* rogue, whom we *should like* to perceive at first hand" (257). Workers also admire criminals because they enjoy the products of their labors. Legal jobs in capitalism rarely provide that satisfaction. When engaged in something illegal, people of all social classes mix without discrimination. Crichton shows this in the scene of the illegal rat-baiting (49–55). The gamblers enjoy genuine interest despite the legal risks. This expression of their true nature becomes a great social equalizer in the manner Marx suggested. These people labor at what they love instead of merely seeking money. Because of that, a classless and cooperative society develops. This contrasts sharply with the broader picture of a society that has begun to destroy itself with a love of wealth.

While these events occurred in the mid-nineteenth century, the novel appeared and became popular in the late twentieth. What does the novel indicate about the culture from which it sprang? A Marxist view of *The Great Train Robbery* would suggest that the popularity of this novel in the twentieth century indicates oncoming disaster for our capitalistic society. This story succeeded in the mid-twentieth century because it represented something our American culture admires. Twentieth-century audiences admire the bravado and intelligence of the mastermind Pierce. Both the novel and its film version gained wide audiences and enthusiastic reviews. The novel even won a Mystery Writers of America Award for best novel of the year in 1975. While our moral attitudes require condemnation of crime, our capitalistic attitudes applaud ingenuity in the spirit of making money. If such a caper is carried out with little or no violence, it becomes even more admirable. As Crichton remarks, crime is "secretly admired, and we are always eager to hear the details of some outstanding criminal exploit" (xvi). Perhaps we vicariously enjoy our own fantasies about control and wealth this way. Pierce pursues wealth not because he needs it but because he wants it. He has no reason other than pure greed. His labor and his reward are intimately connected, and he achieves what he pursues. However, the novel's concern with the pursuit of wealth at all costs addresses a problem that has grown even greater since 1855. Even as the wealthy capitalists struggle to earn more money, they have lost control over the increasing numbers of poor. Crime and violence, motivated by the greed for material wealth and power, have permeated business and government. They have taken over whole neighborhoods and driven fear and distrust into every community in this nation.

Americans fail, as did the Victorians, to recognize the true cause of this problem not as poverty, but as capitalism. As Crichton points out, even today people still view crime as the result of "poverty, injustice, or poor education" (xv). However, it is not need, but the desperate desire for wealth at all costs that drives crime.

6

Eaters of the Dead
(1976)

Crichton's 1976 novel, *Eaters of the Dead*, is perhaps the least popular and the least critically acclaimed of all his fictional works. Critical comments include: "Good try, but what was Crichton thinking?" (Goldner, 4). It has been classified as a book that "no one's ever heard of" (Burchill, 25). Certainly it is unique. This tale of medieval Vikings fighting cannibalistic mist monsters seems a far cry from *The Andromeda Strain* and *Jurassic Park*. This chapter discusses many of the characteristics that make this novel stand out. Its literary and historical context and the development of character through complex points of view make the novel rich. Plot structure ties this novel tightly to the conventions of gothic fiction rather than to adventure or science fiction. Its contemporary theme speaks out on cultural prejudice. The critical reading of the novel introduces deconstruction and suggests how a literary critic using this theory might view *Eaters of the Dead*.

LITERARY AND HISTORICAL CONTEXT

Eaters of the Dead has a particularly interesting and potentially confusing literary and historical background. The novel sets itself up as a scholarly edition of a piece of nonfiction when in fact it is neither scholarly nor nonfiction. However, it is a little bit of both. The "scholarship" portions of the novel consist of an introduction, footnotes, appendix, and bibliography put together by an editor. While some of the references and information contained in them are real, many are not. Crichton makes them up, using an academic style. For instance, one of the sources he cites—Azhared's *Necronomican*—is an imaginary work used by amateur demonologists in the tales of H. P. Lovecraft (Sullivan). So the very parts of the story that present themselves as unquestionably nonfiction are often fictionalized. This causes confusion as readers wonder whether each footnote is genuine. This use of fictionalized scholarship is a unique example of Crichton's usual attention to detail. In other novels he produces computer printouts, maps, and coded messages to add to the scientific realism of his story. However, in this story, set in a pretechnological era, Crichton had to produce pretechnological "documentation" to create that same realism. The novel is stuffed with verisimilitude, or details that make the fiction seem real. The introduction traces the history of the Fadlan manuscript. The appendix discusses the academic debate regarding the survival of Neanderthal man into historic times. And a bibliography lists primary, secondary, and reference sources. The effectiveness of the technique in this novel is debatable. At least one critic argues that "this straining toward verisimilitude becomes a pedantic mannerism" (Sullivan, 22) which destroys the adventurous plot of the book.

In addition, the book is a novel—a work of fiction. But it *is* based, in part, on an actual nonfiction manuscript. A travel account written by Ibn Fadlan does exist, and it inspired the setting of Crichton's tale. Crichton acknowledges his debt to this text in a note on the copyright page of his novel. He writes, "The material contained in the first three chapters is substantially derived from the manuscript of Ibn Fadlan," and he thanks the translators involved. From this we can assume that the material after Chapter 3, or beyond the first encounter with the Vikings, is not part of the real Fadlan manuscript.

The rest of Crichton's book also follows an ancient text, a work of heroic fiction. *Beowulf*, whose author is unknown, is the oldest surviving long poem in English. It is traditionally believed to have been composed in the first half of the eighth century. Set in the first half of the sixth century, it focuses on the Scandinavian forebears of the Anglo-Saxons who later migrated to England. Beowulf is a young noble. He must fight an evil monster who terrorizes the land of King Hrothgar. Eventually, Beowulf must kill the monster's mother as well. Crichton's debt to this book is immense. He uses many of the same names, incidents, and events. Even details from *Beowulf*, like the terror that animals have of the place where Grendel lives, reappear in *Eaters of the Dead*. For instance, in both stories, deer will be torn to pieces by hounds rather than run into the desert of dread. However, Crichton's work does add much to *Beowulf*, particularly through Ibn Fadlan, an Arab observer who comments on the actions of the Scandinavian heroes.

The gothic genre is the part of Crichton's literary heritage that most influences *Eaters of the Dead*. It inspires Crichton's creation of terror for his characters and an unsettling experience for readers. The multiple viewpoints of the characters create a layering of texts. The layering of texts in *Eaters of the Dead* disrupts readers' confidence that the story they read is the one Ibn Fadlan wrote. The innermost text is Fadlan's first person account of events, but the accuracy of this text is continually called into question by the editorial voice. This disruption begins in the introduction when the editor admits that the original manuscript has long been lost. Evidently the editor has reconstructed this version from fragments that have been preserved in later sources (1). These later sources have all passed through translation from their original languages into English. The topmost layer of the novel is this editor, who also changes the text. The explanation of this textual history is meant to provide verisimilitude, a sense that the text is true and has been painstakingly handled by those involved. However, far from calming readers into an unblinking acceptance of the text, the layering confuses the story and its readers. Instead of a solid core of text surrounded by a framework of editorial commentary, we actually have a patchwork narrative, with each patch contributed by a different person who might have altered Fadlan's text. Suddenly, what seemed like a reliable traveler's firsthand account of his adventures becomes a mishmash of confusion, all of which must be considered carefully to determine its truth. Such textual disruption often happens in gothic fiction. It occurs in nearly all the influential classics of the genre, including *Melmoth the Wanderer*, *Frankenstein*, and *Dracula*. Much of the confusion conveyed in the plot is mirrored in the structure of the text. Readers experience their own anxiety dealing with a story that continually seems to slip out of their grasp.

CHARACTER DEVELOPMENT

As in many of Crichton's novels, character development in *Eaters of the Dead* is of little importance compared to plot. The Arabic narrator,

Ibn Fadlan, however, and the editor who prepares Fadlan's text do develop personalities and points of view which influence readers. Beyond these two, however, there are no outstanding characters. None of the Norsemen stand out as individuals. Even the heroic leader Buliwyf evolves as little more than the sum of his battles. Similarly, the wendol remain only a group.

Without a doubt, the most important character in *Eaters of the Dead* is Ibn Fadlan, the young man from Bagdad who travels with the Vikings. His eyewitness account is this text, as the subtitle indicates: "The Manuscript of Ibn Fadlan, Relating His Experiences with the Northmen in A.D. 922." The novel consists almost entirely of Fadlan's first person point of view. It is a story told by a character within the events who refers to himself as "I" in the narrative. This point of view proves particularly important to both the structure of the plot and the development of theme.

The first three chapters—those derived from Fadlan's actual manuscript—are written in a detached, journalistic style. As a result, they often seem dry. They list Islamic settlements. They count the days travelers spent in each place. They complain about the weather. Fadlan's descriptions of the first alien people he meets—the Oguz Turks—are fact-filled anthropological observations. He quickly sketches the tribe's style of housing, religion, form of government, personal cleanliness, hospitality code, laws and punishments, inheritance, and funerary practices. Even Fadlan himself remains personally indistinct.

Once he travels with and learns about the Norsemen, Fadlan begins to reflect and write about *himself*. Here the first person point of view expands to truly include Fadlan's personality. No longer is he a detached observer, but someone who reacts emotionally to the world around him. He also studies his own actions in contrast to those of the strangers he lives with. For example, Fadlan openly admits his own pride after the first successful battle with the wendol. "I am abashed now to think upon my strutting" (97). He describes his fear of heights. "I should rather . . . to eat the excrement of a pig, to put out my eyes, even to die itself" (149–150) than climb a cliff. These show a growing self-awareness that renders the novel increasingly interesting. For it is really the story of this particular Arab's interactions with the Vikings, not the dry list of events, that gives the novel its interest.

The second character whose point of view shapes *Eaters of the Dead* is the fictional editor. This scholarly character has supposedly provided this reconstruction of Fadlan's text for us to read, complete with footnotes, introduction, appendix, and bibliography. That editor evidently is *not* Michael Crichton. Crichton's fictionalization of the materials in the editorial apparatus clearly renders it part of the novel. Therefore, the editor himself is an unnamed character in *Eaters of the Dead*. This editor begins, ends, and continually intrudes into Ibn Fadlan's narrative, controlling it in a way that may change or ruin parts of it. From the start, the editor influences readers' views of Fadlan. The editor calls him smart, but unusual, possibly not trustworthy (8). The editor omits parts of the manuscript. He inserts explanations that direct readers' interpretations of some events. And he controls readers' parting thoughts with his own theory about the nature of the wendol, suggesting that they are actually surviving members of Neanderthal man (177). This anatomical variant of modern man predated Cro-Magnon man and supposedly disappeared over 35,000 years ago. Because of the editor, readers must question the integrity of Fadlan's first person manuscript. Obviously the editor has interfered with it. So how much of the original is left for readers? The editor's character raises our suspicion that the story has been altered or remains incomplete. This is distinctly gothic in tone.

Though indistinct as individuals, the Vikings stand out as a group. They are a boisterous society full of camaraderie and devotion. Relationships to family members, townsfolk, fellow warriors, and kings are sacred. The hero, Buliwyf, answers the call of his relatives, who are losing a battle against the murderous mist monsters. He and his band of warriors willingly head north, where they face the dreaded wendol. Their calm view of injury and death continues the classic heroic tradition. In ancient Greek works, heroes did not fear death. Instead they feared the dishonor of dying unknown, without encountering the glories of war. This is also true of the Vikings. The terror these brave and hearty men feel when faced with such seemingly harmless things as mist and broken statues frightens readers as well.

The antagonists of this novel, or the characters who fight against the heroes, are the mysterious wendol. They are hideous, inarticulate cannibals of incredible bravery, ferocity, and strength. The Vikings and the Arab narrator all consider them nonhuman creatures. However, the book reveals that the horrifying and satanic wendol may not be distinctly "other" creatures after all. In fact, they may represent some element of humanity. If the wendol are Neanderthal man, thought to be extinct for many thousands of years, then they represent a gruesome return of some undesirable element of ourselves thought forever out of reach. The Norse say that the wendol have been missing for at least four generations.

Many of the Vikings had stopped believing in them (88). The implications for potential horrors are tremendous. What else lies in our past, either as a race or as individuals, that might someday reappear and violently disrupt our lives? Every individual has hidden secrets, potential violence, and contained emotions that he or she fears to let out. In *Eaters of the Dead*, the wendol represent those dangerous elements.

PLOT DEVELOPMENT

In *Eaters of the Dead*, the plot's conflict develops as the heroic Vikings clash with the evil wendol. Many writers use short, exciting episodes in their plots to create suspense and drive an adventure story forward. However, many episodes in *Eaters of the Dead* feel unconnected, and therefore the book is less powerful. The early part of Fadlan's narrative is largely a catalogue of customs, and not until the Norse pursue the wendol do the episodes begin to connect. Prior to that, no intense conflict shapes the narrative.

Conflict begins as Fadlan and his readers puzzle over the brave and stoic Norsemen's terror of things that appear harmless. As they journey back to their leader Buliwyf's childhood home, the sailors brave encounters with sea monsters but shrink from a simple mist (72). To them, the mist symbolizes some other source of fear. So terrific is their terror that the Vikings cannot even name the thing they fear, and Fadlan and his readers remain mystified. When the group follows strange footprints, they walk slowly, dreading something Fadlan cannot understand (76). The Norsemen's terror arises again when they find a piece of carved stone. This depiction of the torso of a pregnant female, which Fadlan evaluates as primitive and harmless (78), sends the Norse into uncontrollable fright. "The Northmen were suddenly overcome and pale and tremulous . . . then were several of the warriors sick, and purged themselves upon the ground. And the general horror was very great, to my mystification" (78). This produces the feeling, in both Fadlan and readers, that the Norse clearly know something we don't about this evil enemy, and our anxiety and curiosity rise.

The conflict between the Norse protagonists and the murderous wendol emerges when the Norse arrive at Buliwyf's home and find the village destroyed, the inhabitants murdered. At this point, the tale becomes even more gothic in feel. In gothic fiction, antagonists exceed the bounds of the ordinary in every way. They present more than an obstacle to the heroes' desires. They are a horrific evil against which goodness and rationality are ineffective. This is the case with the wendol, who murder people with remarkable savagery, dismembering and gnawing on corpses, and stealing their victims' heads as trophies.

Buliwyf's band travels to the kingdom of Rothgar to help him battle the wendol, who have begun to attack his people. At this point, gothic elements recede and the adventure plot takes over as a desperate war unfolds. During the skirmishes, we get our first glimpse of these mysterious and frightening creatures. Their appearance, as described by Fadlan, is appalling.

> I heard a low grunting sound, like the rooting of a pig . . . and I smelled a rank odor like the rot of a carcass after a month. . . . I saw eyes that shown like fire. . . . I remember, most distinctly, the touch of these monsters upon me, especially the furry aspect of the bodies, for these mist monsters have hair as long as a hairy dog, and as thick, on all parts of their bodies. (90–91)

In battle after battle the Norse suffer tremendous losses, but continue to fight their enemy with almost superhuman vigor and bravery.

Eventually, the Norsemen decide that in order to eliminate the wendol forever, they must attack the wendol's central stronghold, the home of their mother-wife. Their passage through the desert of dread, down a towering cliff, and through submerged tunnels tests the physical and mental strength of all the characters. Fadlan, though terrified, survives to see the final encounter. Once in the thunder caves, Buliwyf battles his way to the mother's chamber, where he and the creature stab each other mortally. She dies on the spot. Buliwyf lives only long enough to return to Rothgar's fortress, where he will receive proper funeral honors.

The novel's final development, contained in the "scholarly" appendix, returns the novel to gothic conventions, leaving readers with an irreconcilable fear. The appendix presents "scientific theories" that the mist monsters described in Fadlan's text are Neanderthal men, suggesting that Neanderthals lived alongside modern humans (177). Though the appendix also presents opposing viewpoints, the editor clearly favors the wendol-as-human-ancestor theory. This provides the typical gothic ending: an enduring anxiety that stays with the reader after finishing the book. If these supposedly long lost creatures still exist among us, what other long forgotten terrors may reappear at any time?

The novel also presents its two main characters, Ibn Fadlan and the fictional editor, in conflict, for each represents a different perspective on the implications of the wendol's similarity to humanity. The novel challenges its audience not to ignore these ideas. The Northmen ignored the wendol for four generations, and suffered tremendously. Crichton wants his audience to acknowledge the terrors that lie within our own deserts of dread. Fadlan fails to do this. Instead, he protects himself from his own honest observations and the fears they bring. Every time Fadlan notices that the wendol resemble humans, he insists they are not humanlike at all. For instance, he describes the shape of their footprints as "human, yet not human" (76), and when he sees them he describes their shapes as "hardly in the manner of men, yet also manlike" (90). He cannot face the possibility that humans hold this violent potential within them. The editor, however, subtly pokes fun at the common human tendency to turn a blind eye to things abhorrent to us. In his final line in the novel he remarks, "One may adopt whatever stance satisfies an inner sense of the fitness of things" (179). His statement clearly laughs at the concept of truth. He acknowledges that people will see only what is acceptable to their existing world view. This relativity of perception based on fear adds to the distinctly gothic flavor of this novel.

THEMATIC ISSUES

This gothic concept of the relativity of perception is the main theme of *Eaters of the Dead*. Because people often acknowledge only that which is acceptable to their existing world view, anything conceived of as distinctly different is ignored, rejected, feared, or destroyed. This is ethnocentrism—a preference for the characteristics of a culture or race based merely on familiarity. It is also prejudice. *Eaters of the Dead* suggests that such ethnocentrism limits people's ability to cope with situations by causing illogical and often dangerous attitudes.

In the appendix, the editor quotes a statement by E. D. Goodrich of the University of Philadelphia that points out the thematic significance of this novel: "To untrained observers, cultural differences are often interpreted as physical differences. . . . Thus, as late as the 1880's it was possible for educated Europeans to wonder aloud whether Negroes in primitive African societies could be considered human beings at all, or whether they represented some bizarre mating of men and apes" (178). This is also true of Fadlan's initial assessment of the Norsemen and of their assessment, in turn, of the wendol. Both of the other groups are so different from the Arab that he sees them as somehow inhuman, and therefore of less value. Even in the introduction, the editor discusses how historians traditionally dismiss the Vikings as barbarous invaders, with little culture of their own. A more open-minded approach, however, recognizes the value of that society's burial grounds, stonework, and other accomplishments. This traditional discounting of any culture not based on Greece or Rome is simply ethnocentrism. Western culture views the others as different and therefore underdeveloped.

The ridiculousness of such ethnocentrism is clearly illustrated in the novel as Fadlan joins the Norsemen to fight a common enemy. Fadlan initially viewed the Norsemen as backward and foul: "the filthiest race that God ever created" (31). But in a few weeks Fadlan feels like one of them. For instance, he pauses in his work to rape a slave woman, as the Norse do (98). When his group saves Hurot hall, he rejoices as if he were a Northman (118). When wounded he determines to show a Northman's cheer (121). The night before the attack on the wendol caves he reports, "That night I felt I had been born a Northman" (143). Even the Norse captain, Buliwyf, notes Fadlan's changed attitude, charging him to live and write about their adventures because he is more a Northman than an Arab (145). What causes this complete shift in attitude? Fadlan himself recognizes it and explains: "strange things cease to be strange upon repetition" (129). Ethnocentrism is like any other prejudice, born of a fear of the unknown and destroyed through familiarity and security. Often, however, the prejudice prevents that familiarity from ever developing. Like Fadlan, many people would rather die than learn about what they fear. With this book Crichton clearly advises against such fears. He encourages his readers to approach other cultures and races in a more open-minded fashion.

A DECONSTRUCTIONIST READING OF *EATERS OF THE DEAD*

Deconstruction theory is founded on an idea many of us have experienced when reading, or watching the news, or listening to political debate (Murfin, "Deconstruction," 266). At some time, we have all witnessed someone arguing about an issue and realized that he is leaving out important information. Other possibilities exist. The argument simply won't stand up against good questioning. In fact, we sometimes realize that the evidence could also support an opposing argument. That is the same basic critical activity that deconstruction promotes. Deconstruction sets out to prove that texts can often support multiple readings. In fact, the same text can validly be used to argue exactly opposite meanings. There is no single truth to any text, but many interpretations.

Deconstruction has its beginnings in linguistics and philosophy. Ferdinand de Saussure and, following him, Jacques Derrida, explored the way we understand the meanings of words and ideas. Both believed that distinction or difference between different things, words, and ideas gives them clear meaning. In other words, we understand the concept of light because we also understand the concept of dark. If we did not have opposites or differences in meanings, the words would be valueless. We would not understand, or even have, the concept of cold if we did not also experience heat. Thus every word or idea relies on its opposite to create the difference that gives it its meaning. Every word or idea incorporates its opposite with every use. This understanding of the relationship between opposites opens up new meanings by sparking a new awareness of the oppositions within a text.

However, when society evaluates any pair of opposites, it inevitably values one member of the pair more than the other. For instance, in the pairings male/female, active/passive, rich/poor, civilized/uncivilized, the first item in each pair is traditionally valued as superior to the second. However, deconstruction acts against such valuing of one option over another. Since meaning is contained in opposition, Derrida argues that neither side of such a split could be valued over another because they could not exist without each other. Such prejudice is in error.

Deconstruction argues that literary texts fall into the same pattern. They present oppositions and value one item in the pair over the other. However, because meaning comes from opposition, any text that states a theme must also contain the opposite idea. Selden and Widdowson point out that "deconstruction can begin when we locate the moment when a text *transgresses the laws it appears to set up for itself*" (147). In other words, when the text seems to contradict itself, deconstruction can start. This location destroys the valuing of one idea over another. Steven Lynn explains that to deconstruct a text one must "locate an opposition, determine which member is privileged, then reverse and undermine the hierarchy" (263). This is what we shall attempt to do for Michael Crichton's *Eaters of the Dead*.

The opposition central to *Eaters of the Dead* is easy to locate. The novel clearly presents the opposition between ethnocentrism and open-minded evaluation of foreign societies. This dilemma faces every character in the book. Arabs, Vikings, and wendol all encounter each other. They have to choose how they will react. They can try to learn about each other. Or they can assume that the different cultures are of less value than their own and therefore prime targets for annihilation. This same choice faces the novel's readers as well.

This opposition rests on another: civilized versus primitive societies. Here "civilized" means a society with refined manner and tastes. This, however, is a completely subjective judgment, based on the cultural practice with which one is familiar. For instance, Norse and Arabs regard each other as vulgar when it comes to burying the dead. The Norse, who come from a cold, wet climate, cremate their dead. They believe this hastens the entry into Paradise. Burial would allow the beloved's body to be devoured by worms (38). Arabs, many of whom come from arid areas, bury their dead to preserve the body for the day of judgment, when it will rise. Each views the other with ridicule. How, then, does one determine which is more "refined" in manner and taste? The judgment is screened through a prejudice based on one's own belief system, or ethnocentrism.

Eaters of the Dead clearly values open-minded evaluation of another culture over judgment based on cultural prejudice, noting the lack of rationality in ethnocentric views. In the introduction, the editor calls the traditional historical view of the Vikings exaggerated, bloodcurdling, and illogical (4). He explains the often ridiculous views of the Vikings as the result of "a long-standing European bias" (5) which has "civilization" spreading northward from the Roman world. This view is proven wrong by objective carbon-dating techniques, which show that massive stone tombs, metallurgy, and astronomy all developed in the Northland *before* they developed in the "civilized" world (6). Cultural prejudice kept Western scholars from appreciating the accomplishments of Viking culture.

As described in the section on theme, Ibn Fadlan initially experiences a similar prejudice against the Northmen. He overcomes this, however, as he grows more familiar with the Viking way of life. Eventually he dresses, talks, and fights like a Viking. The Norse leader even trusts the Arab to tell his tale. This is no small matter to the captain, who believes that his immortality relies on his fame after death. This acceptance results from Fadlan's loss of prejudice. He gains an ability to judge the details of the foreign society objectively on the basis of their value, not because of their difference. Ultimately this attitude makes Fadlan happier. He had considered himself no better than a dead man when he first joined the Norse group. Now he finds himself surrounded by friends, proven in valor, and rich in experience.

Despite the strength of this theme, *Eaters of the Dead* actually contradicts itself and fails to condemn ethnocentric bias. Although the Arab and the Norse evaluate each other fairly, Crichton never suggests that such a nonprejudicial approach should be extended to the wendol. Objectivity and open-mindedness are given only to other cultures that *deserve* such consideration. But this is a prejudgment that stems from cultural prejudice. The book fails to act out its own message against prejudice when it unflinchingly condemns the most foreign society of all.

An objective view of the wendol society reveals no logical reason for their exclusion. True, they are killers. But their murderous attacks on Viking farms and villages are like the raids Vikings launched on vulnerable Europeans. Therefore, the wendol's warlike ways, though certainly hated by their enemies, do not justify condemnation. Their physical appearance is no more shocking than the Vikings' initially seemed to Fadlan. Many things about the Norsemen's bodies, food, and customs offended his senses as severely as the wendol did. Had Fadlan lived with the wendol for several months, would his opinion of them have changed as dramatically as did his opinion of the Vikings? The texts provides a hint: "I no longer attended the hideous stench of the wendol, for I had been smelling it a goodly time" (129–130).

One thing does render the wendol society different from the others, so different that it cannot be accepted. That difference appears in the Vikings' reactions to wendol worship. While the sight of decapitated, gnawed bodies draws little reaction from the Norse, a crudely carved statue of a pregnant female torso renders them nauseated with terror (78, 121). This is the image of the mother who governs the wendol (121). Thus, when the Norse set out against the wendol, it is not enough to conquer them. The Norse must completely destroy them and their homes (138).

The wendol society is a matriarchy, a society run by women. This makes the wendol unacceptable to patriarchal societies run by men, like the Arab and Viking cultures. This gap stretches wider than Arab versus Viking, city-dweller versus nomad, artistic and literate versus militaristic and illiterate, monotheistic versus polytheistic. Wendol matriarchy is too different from the Arab and Norse societies, where men rule and women serve largely as sexual slaves (14, 22, 32, 37, 98, etc.). Laws and customs, though quite different in the Arab and Norse worlds, all are based on the assumption of male primacy. The matriarchal wendol apparently have no basis of similarity with the other societies. Thus they are too foreign to earn anything but loathing and, ultimately, destruction.

This condemnation of the wendol shows that ethnocentrism is, in fact, present and accepted in Crichton's book. Though the theme apparently values open-mindedness, this is ultimately only practiced in certain situations. Thus, that prejudice underlies the entire novel, despite its apparent theme. The values the novel wishes to present deconstruct when the text is examined closely.

Deconstruction suggests that *Eaters of the Dead*, often regarded as Crichton's worst novel, does include interesting technical and theoretical issues worth discussing. This reading also leads to a feminist exploration into why this matriarchal society receives such violent treatment in this novel. Readers may want to see Chapters 4 and 11 for the discussion of feminism and explore those possibilities for themselves.

7

Sphere
(1987)

"I think the only true expression of one's beliefs lies in action," writes Michael Crichton in his autobiography, *Travels* (251). His 1987 novel, *Sphere*, shows what happens when one's beliefs and desires become reality. Set 1,000 feet below the surface of the Pacific Ocean, *Sphere* brings a small team of naval and civilian personnel into contact with a gigantic spaceship. The spaceship, which has been submerged for at least three centuries, reveals one new mystery after another. The most arresting of these is a thirty-foot-wide silver sphere covered with alien designs and without apparent purpose. Crichton's exploration of how humans deal with this situation reveals that many aspects of our own environment are alien to us. This chapter looks at Crichton's expert creation of a suspenseful plot and his presentation of characters who suffer from a variety of resentments. From this, he develops a theme about the nature of power that neatly parallels psychological analysis.

PLOT DEVELOPMENT

Readers speed through Michael Crichton's novels with nervous delight because of his suspenseful plots. *Sphere* is no exception. Crichton combines three literary techniques with plot development to create the powerful tension of this psychological thriller. The events of the plot are shaped through Crichton's selection of point of view. His creation of verisimilitude, or realistic detail, enhances the believability of the events. Finally, Crichton uses the "ticking clock" technique to make episodes race to the book's conclusion. As *Book World* reported, "It's all WHAM! BOOM! BASH! for Norman and company" (Collins, 14).

The events and conflicts of *Sphere*'s plot are all filtered through the perspective of the novel's central character. The book opens with Norman Johnson, a psychologist in his fifties, speeding by military helicopter to the site of what he thinks is a mid-ocean plane crash. He soon discovers, however, that the submerged craft is not a plane but a giant spaceship, that has been there for at least 300 years. The Navy wants him and a team of other experts in math, biology, and astrophysics to live in an undersea habitat while they study the ship. Their undersea explorations soon reveal the only significant cargo on the ship to be a mysterious sphere, which grants certain people the power to make things they imagine come true.

Reader interest and tension grow primarily because of the audience's close connection to Norman. Every conflict in the novel features him. Norman must battle the dangers of the undersea environment and the mysteries of the sphere to do his job for the Navy. But he must also battle his colleagues' hostilities and his own fears. Through the power of the sphere, these emotional obstacles become physical ones that threaten to kill everyone in the habitat. Only Norman has the ability to withstand these conflicts and to triumph over each powerful obstacle. In many ways, this plot pattern resembles that of the prototypical adventure story, discussed in Chapters 2 and 8.

Crichton's depiction of events is limited to what Norman observes or does. This is called the limited omniscient point of view. This writing technique focuses readers on the actions and thoughts of a single character, in this case, the central character. This technique achieves a variety of effects. Often, authors focus their limited omniscience on a likable, rather average central character, like Norman. This encourages audiences to bond closely with the story. Because readers relate easily to Norman, they care about what happens to him. Also, readers find out only what the central character knows or suspects. Thus, as Norman continually finds himself surrounded by threatening circumstances, readers feel as if they are there with him. Events that terrify or surprise him have the same effect on audiences.

Crichton's descriptions of these terrifying events also enhance the effect of the plot. Norman simply wants to solve the mystery of the sphere and return safely to the earth's surface. But as *Sphere* progresses, Norman (and along with him, the reader) encounters antagonists of increasing strength. First, a violent storm forces the support and rescue ships to leave the area, essentially isolating the team on the bottom of the ocean. Then some unknown but apparently intelligent life form (which calls itself Jerry) begins to communicate with them. Jerry exhibits a dangerously volatile personality, behaving like a toddler when unhappy or angry. In throwing his tantrums, however, Jerry becomes a giant squid and attacks the undersea habitat and its occupants. One life support system after another suffers damage, until the team can barely survive inside the habitat.

Crichton makes these conflicts come alive by depicting the situations with vivid technological detail, or verisimilitude. His skill at explaining accurate and technical detail so that the average reader can understand it enhances all of his novels. In *Sphere*, for instance, the Navy wants to test its undersea habitats for an extended period of time. Crichton "renders the nuts and bolts of the habitat with accuracy, skill, and verisimilitude," reports one critic (Spinrad, 101). This description makes readers claustrophobic along with Norman as he struggles to adjust to his new surroundings. Instead, the conflict grows more intense as he finds himself more uncomfortable with time. This technique is typical Crichton, developed from the long history established by science fiction and thriller novels.

Crichton's use of verisimilitude also heightens the conflict between the humans and the monster from the sphere. His information about marine biology, the space/time continuum, black holes, and advanced metallurgy scare and confuse readers and characters alike. Reproductions of computer monitors and printouts enable readers to enter the action. We see for ourselves what the characters view as they try to decode complex messages and struggle against violent sea monsters. Understanding the issues and dangers involved in the characters' predicament increases reader anxiety as adventures develop.

As the plot plummets through one deadly situation after another, Crichton turns up the emotional pressure for his readers by employing a technique known as the ticking clock. To do this, an author sets an imaginary timer that indicates the inescapable approach of some event. Crichton introduces this several times, and with increasingly minute increments, thus building the characters'—and the readers'—desperation. Crichton's first clock counts time in days, marking the progress of the Pacific storm that has forced the support ships for the undersea operation to leave the area. Until the ships return, the main characters cannot escape the deep. Norman continually reminds himself (and thus readers) of how many more days they must endure before rescue is possible (233). As danger heightens, so does the importance of time. Crichton emphasizes this with a radio message announcing that help for the habitat will arrive in sixteen hours. Even then, Norman doubts they can survive that long (278). The last 100 pages of *Sphere* emphasize the slow passage of time by abandoning conventional chapter headings. The new chapter headings count down the time remaining until the rescue.

The final ticking clock set by Crichton is the most focused. Crazed by her contact with the sphere, one of the scientists has armed a collection of demolition explosives to destroy the undersea compound. A mini-sub tethered a short distance from the habitat serves as their taxi to the surface in calm weather, and now it provides the only chance for escape. As the survivors attempt to board the mini-sub and escape the impending blast, the clock commands the narrative. "Harry was counting: 'Five twenty-nine . . . five twenty-eight . . . ' he was thinking they were in terrible trouble . . . 'Forty seconds . . . We'll never make it' " (354–357). This focus on limited time, coupled with the details and the clearly expressed terror of the characters, builds to a climax that captures readers in an inescapable grip.

Only Norman and two of the original team members return safely to the surface, where they are rescued by the newly returned Navy fleet. Even there, however, they face a challenge. They must decide the best course of action to take regarding the spaceship and the sphere, which still lie on the ocean floor. As scientists, they long to reveal their new discoveries, but as humans who have suffered under the sphere's power, they need to prevent further pain and death. Isolated in a decompression chamber, the three agree to hide their knowledge forever, hoping to spare the world more misery. Crichton's conclusion is deftly handled, tying up every thread of the plot but leaving thematic issues open for further exploration.

CHARACTER DEVELOPMENT

Within this skillfully developed thriller moves a collection of unique characters. Together, they make up an interesting portrait of American society. The strangeness and isolation of their undersea environment highlight the unique aspects of each character. However, though each is distinct, they all share one trait: all feel resentment toward some outside force that they think has victimized them. Ultimately, though, these resentments negatively affect the characters themselves.

Each of the four central characters is unique in an almost exaggerated way. Zoologist Beth Halpern is the only female on the undersea team, even though research has revealed that women perform better in contained environments than men (58–59). She is highly aware of her status, as are the men. This awareness is heightened by everyone's frequent references to gender. Harry Adams is a thirty-year-old black mathematician. He was a child genious whose uniqueness was emphasized as he grew up in a ghetto. The third unique personality is an astrophysicist whose head is always in the stars. Ted Fielding worries more about filming the historic moments of their adventure and writing his memoirs than he does about surviving the ordeal. Finally, Norman Johnson, the central character, is unique because of his averageness. This fifty-three-year-old family man squabbles with his wife, worries about car repairs, dreams of retirement, and struggles with a bulging waistline. He becomes nervous in the mini-sub and finds the habitat cold and unnatural. While the adventure intrigues him, he would rather not be on it because its dangers terrify him.

Despite the variety in their backgrounds and abilities, all these characters are loaded with resentment and anxiety. They all believe that they have been victimized by sources beyond their control. Beth feels that men prevent her from achieving what she deserves. She accuses Barnes of treating her poorly because she is female (95), and decries Harry's attitude (252). In her eyes the men always stick together and exclude her (96). Her generalized resentment comes from a failed love affair with a professor. He not only dumped her, but published her research under his name (96–97). As a result, she desires the power men seem to possess. She makes up for what she sees as her lack by building up her physical strength (24) and her physical attraction (266). Clearly, Beth feels anxious because she does not have the power she thinks she needs. Crichton also examines women's desire for power in *The Terminal Man* and *Disclosure*.

Similarly, Harry Adams feels that he cannot succeed in society as well as an equally talented white man could. He is quick to assume that the other characters' treatment of him is racially motivated, even when such assumptions are patently ridiculous. For instance, when Barnes lists all the scientists by naming them from left to right, Harry quickly assumes he is last because he is black (71). His hasty accusations, however, create the very thing he fears. Wrongly accused, the others develop negative feelings toward him. They avoid Harry, not because he is black, but because he cannot forgive them for being white.

Ted Fielding, the open, pompous, preppie, happy-go-lucky, camera-hungry astrophysicist, seems charmingly irrepressible. Ultimately, though, he proves to be driven by hated forces beyond his control. In fact, he competes strongly with Harry Adams, jealously loathing the younger man's phenomenal professional success. "He's so arrogant. . . . And on top of that, he's young!" (150). The forty-year-old scientist clearly suffers from a classic mid-life crisis. "He clung to his youth out of a sense that time was slipping by and he hadn't yet accomplished anything" (150). He even carries a photograph of a red Corvette in his scientific journal.

Next to the others, psychologist Norman Johnson seems remarkably well adjusted, but even he harbors resentments from a time when he felt victimized. His enemies are scientists who deal only with scientific fads. When Norman was young, people thought his research brilliant. But when psychological fashion shifted to drug therapy, they forgot him (13). As a result, his professional and financial stability suffered. Since then, Norman has worried about the value of his work. He has also hated the types of professionals who caused this instability (313). He feels similarly underrated throughout the undersea adventure. He worries about the legitimacy of his work and his inclusion on the team from the moment he has trouble fitting his paunch through the submarine hatch (47). Norman's desire to control his environment and thereby establish his legitimacy within it becomes ever more prominent as the novel progresses.

Analysis of all these characters reveals that, through resentment and anxiety, each brings himself into great danger. As with the traditional concept of the self-fulfilling prophecy, the anxieties become realities. Thus many of the self-doubts prove true. Beth hates men who treat her as unworthy, but she hates herself even more because she feels she may actually be unworthy. With "a deep core of self-hate . . . Beth saw herself as a victim who struggled against her fate. . . . She failed to see how she had done it to herself" (321). Harry, the mathematician who lives in a world of the abstract, accuses other people of abandoning him as a freak when ultimately it is he who avoids relationships (321). Ted fears that the professional world will never appreciate him. Yet when given the chance to speak, he does so only through stolen quotations. The ultimate plagiarist, Ted is too fearful to produce anything original. His final attempts to reproduce the alien's communications end in disaster. And Norman's fear of being a fifth wheel drives him into silence. By not contributing, he indeed becomes of little use to the group. When the others need him, however, he must struggle to escape from this negative self-concept so he can contribute in a life-saving way. These hidden, subconscious motives that drive people's actions figure prominently as the central obstacle in this novel's plot. The characters must overcome them if they are to survive.

THEMATIC ISSUES

In many of his novels, Michael Crichton blends character development with thematic development, often using his cast to dramatize the various aspects of his theme. Chapters 4 and 9 provide additional examples of this technique. In *Sphere*, Crichton uses his character development differently. The characters all actually prove the same thing about the theme, which is the power of fear. This novel makes a simple yet thought-provoking statement about humanity: human greatness lies in our ability to imagine.

Glorifying imagination is a theme that would satisfy any writer. In so doing, Crichton honors his own craft as the defining characteristic of humanity. The entire action of the book testifies to the greatness of human imagination. Humans establish undersea habitats, investigate an alien spacecraft, break codes, and navigate black holes. However, it is Norman's visit to the sphere that provides the first articulation of the theme.

> [No animal can] perform the activity you call imagining. It cannot make mental images of how reality might be. . . . This special ability of imagination is what has made your species as great as it is. Nothing else. It is not your ape-nature, not your tool-using nature, not language or your violence or your caring for young or your social groupings. It is none of these things, which are all found in other animals. Your greatness lies in imagination. . . . imagining it [anything] is what makes it happen. This is the gift of your species and this is the danger, because you do not choose to control your imaginings . . . you take no responsibility for the choice. (335)

For an author like Michael Crichton, this is a fundamental truth. His imaginings have achieved reality in the form of novels, movies, and television shows. He believes that this applies to all people, not just writers and inventors. In a sense it is a new way to encourage people to take responsibility for their own destinies. If you believe you will succeed, or fail, or be victimized, or gain power, eventually you probably will. But Crichton believes that people do not recognize their ability to shape their own lives. Instead, like Beth, Harry, Ted, and Norman, people assume their own innocence and blame others for what happens to them.

This attitude of victimization has grown in American society since *Sphere* was published in 1987. The creative not guilty pleas of the Menendez brothers, Lorena Bobbitt, and others drew much public attention. So did highly publicized cases in which criminals sued their victims for personal injuries. These issues became the topic of national discussion in the 1990s. They appeared on the covers of national magazines and as the focus of network news specials.[1] Feminism came under criticism for promoting the idea of women as natural victims of men. Crichton himself continued to work with the theme of victimization, most notably in his 1994 novel, *Disclosure*.

Norman Johnson, the central character of *Sphere*, faces the powers of his own imagination and ultimately accepts responsibility for the choices he makes. The other survivors, Beth and Harry, remain too caught up in preserving their guilt-free victim status to acknowledge their own imaginings. Therefore, they remain dangerous to themselves and to others. When Beth and Norman try to convince Harry that he has created the murderous "Jerry," he denies it over and over. *"It has nothing to do with me!"* (290). Beth, when faced with her own destructive power, fills with even more self-loathing. Under her influence, the habitat lights grow dim, and a strange green, slimy mold covers the walls (350). As Norman attempts to save her life, she can do nothing but insist that she deserves to die. She almost kills Norman and Harry in the process of achieving what she thinks she deserves.

Norman very nearly falls into the same trap of self-denial. Once he controls the only mini-sub that can take survivors to the surface, he starts to ascend. His visit to the sphere has made his worst fears come to life, as it did for the others. But whereas Harry produced a giant squid and Beth a formless cyclone of power, Norman generates complete confidence and total lack of compassion (341). As he ascends, his new purposeful self struggles to justify its actions to his compassionate self. Though he believes that everyone must take responsibility for his actions, he contradicts himself. He insists he has no choice, no responsibility in what happens to Harry and Beth (343–344). Continuing to float away from the habitat, Norman congratulates himself on his control of his fear, on succeeding where Harry and Beth failed. But suddenly he realizes that something is wrong. As he struggles to deny his realization, he finds himself admitting that he wants only to save himself. He is afraid to die (347). This recognition of his fear strengthens Norman's true sense of self. Though he believes that if he goes back he will probably die, he turns the fleeing sub around. He realizes that abandoning Harry and Beth would have ignored everything he valued (347). He had almost done it, however, because of fear.

Norman's acceptance of the responsibility and control he has over his own situation stands out against society as a whole. In *Sphere*, society is represented by the military. One of Crichton's secondary themes suggests that contemporary society denies problems. The deep sea operation involves cover-ups directed at everyone from the civilian divers to the President of the United States. The naval personnel who exude confidence about running a habitat 1,000 feet below the ocean's surface cannot keep the lights or air conditioning running on a small command ship. And, as Norman observes, "a society in which the most common prescription drug was Valium was . . . a society with unsolved problems" (14). This is a society that works hard to deny the existence of those problems. Crichton addresses this issue of social denial throughout his novels, notably in *The Great Train Robbery* and *Rising Sun*.

A PSYCHOANALYTIC READING OF *SPHERE*

Sphere focuses on the powers of imagination, on the denial of fear and anger, and on the destructive forces these unleash. This leads almost naturally to a psychoanalytic consideration of the novel. The Freudian roots of psychoanalysis, as outlined in Chapter 3, provide a unique insight into *Sphere*. Through the central character, a psychologist, Crichton makes psychology stand out in the novel. However, Norman's theories are based not on Freud, but on one of Freud's disciples, Karl Jung. In explaining the powers of the sphere to Beth, Norman explains Jung's concept of the shadow. "Everybody had a dark side to his personality . . . [which] contained all the unacknowledged personality aspects . . . if you didn't acknowledge your shadow side, it would rule you" (273). This is ultimately a refinement of Freud's concept of the repressed material contained within the unconscious. Because Jung's work is based so closely on Freud, and because Freud's ideas can further illuminate elements of Crichton's work, Freud will be used as the governing framework for this analysis.

The structure of Crichton's novel resembles an outline for Freudian analysis. It tells what these characters will endure and suggests what people might experience if they embark on self-examination. The four main sections of the book are:

1. The Surface
2. The Deep
3. The Monster
4. The Power

These titles suggest a journey through the human mind as defined by Freud. Starting with the ego—the surface self which every person presents to the social world—analysis ventures into the deep world of the unconscious, where the bulk of our personality (including the id and the superego) resides. There, in addition to fabulous wonders, we locate the terrifying repressed materials, those feared desires which people deny, but which never disappear. Once set free, these monstrous elements endanger the surface self, which began the journey. The power unleashed is incredible—and controlling it is no easy task, as *Sphere* shows.

Section I, "The Surface," focuses on appearances, as does the ego portion of the Freudian personality. Literally set on the surface of the Pacific Ocean, this section provides background information on the major characters and on the situation that has brought them here. At this point we know all the characters only at the ego level, seeing only the faces that they have prepared to meet each other. Episodes focus on physical issues: lighting, heat, food, air conditioning, and medical tests. The surface offers plenty of hints about what lies beneath it, but little true information escapes. Even the naval personnel who control the operation don't know everything about what lies beneath. This is also true of the Freudian ego. The conscious self does not remember or acknowledge the contents of the unconsciousness, which buoys it up.

As the people from the surface begin the descent into the deep, the emotions they encounter resemble any one person's first encounters with his own unconscious material. In the deep, time becomes confused and almost irrelevant. This indicator of life on the surface is not valuable here. Under the ocean, the crew lose track of time through their constant contact with undifferentiated darkness. This concept becomes further confused as they encounter a spaceship which has rested on the ocean floor for many centuries, but which clearly comes from earth's future. Similarly, past, present, and future all become distorted in the unconscious. Here repressed materials remain true to their original form. In other words, extreme fear or rage felt by a small child may be repressed because it seems threatening. Thirty years later it will exist in the unconscious in the same form experienced by a five-year-old. This is because repressed material remains locked out of the conscious personality, and as individuals mature and learn to moderate their emotions, they do not moderate their repressed material.

The first response of the surface personalities is to seek reassurance, insisting that the world of the deep is not so strange after all. The habitat in which the characters live is decorated to look as much like the surface world as possible. The facility's cook even promises to make the crew their favorite desserts (59). This decoration of the deep eases the crew— or in the case of analysis, the investigating ego—into the new situation. This allows them to feel comfortable before encountering the true reason for their visit. But ultimately, the differences become inescapable. Eventually, the atmosphere seems dreary and dangerous, held together with heavy bolts and steel plating. The surface realities of time and place fade as the characters begin to contact the realities of the deep.

In the unconscious, waiting for release, lies the monster. This is the Jungian shadow, or the repressed material of Freud's unconscious. This material has been contained in the depths of the unconscious because the conscious personality felt it was too horrifying to acknowledge. This monster is released by a simple acknowledgment. Within the novel, this is a visit to the sphere. Once free, it strives to satisfy its desperate need to communicate. Freud's theory suggests that repressed material initially breaks into the consciousness through dreams. Similarly, the novel's monster initially communicates in code, continually recoding itself until recognized by the surface crew. Once acknowledged, the monster is free to act, childishly satisfying its own needs with little consideration for the others. Norman continually calls the monster a "child king," controlled by immature emotions and free to act without mature (parental) control. Spoiled and demanding, the monster lashes out against any new attempts to control it, announcing "I WILL KILL YOU ALL" (281) when contradicted. This type of murderous rage is typical of small children, who rarely express it because they know how such emotions threaten their own survival. Instead they repress it. But, as Crichton points out, "the irrational side didn't go away if you refused to deal with it. On the contrary, left unattended, the irrational side of man had grown in power" (342).

Once released, the enormous energies of the monster easily overpower the fragile control of the crew from the surface. In a combat for control, the crew—and the ego they represent—will surely lose. Then the monster will reign supreme. In a circular relationship, the monster's threats to break free have created tremendous anxieties in the crew. At the same time, the crew "creates" the monster's dangerous activities to justify their anxieties, which grow even stronger when the monster threatens them. But section IV of *Sphere* illustrates how the energies of the monster can be harnessed and used to achieve positive (not destructive) results.

The power of the monster is the power of all humanity, the ability to make thought real without effort. This ability is what drives humans to repress so many urges that might otherwise become reality. In fact, Crichton suggests that humans have repressed the knowledge of this ability. People actually insist on the opposite (272).

Control of this ability is lost through fear and denial, and can only be regained through an acknowledgment of the monster as part of oneself. About fear, Crichton wrote, "We feel we are afraid to look, when actually it is not-looking that makes us afraid" (*Travels*, 163). Harry and Beth deny their fear, and as a result nearly die, helpless to save themselves. Norman acknowledges his murderous rage at the others and faces his terror of returning to rescue them. He taps the enormous energies of his "monster" by working with it instead of against it (342–347). Empowered, he saves not only himself, but the other two as well.

The final scenes of *Sphere* provide a complex conclusion to this exploration of self-analysis. On one hand, all three of the survivors seem to grasp the power as they discuss their adventures and face their weaknesses. Rationally and cooperatively, they control their thoughts and force themselves to forget everything that might lead other humans to this dangerous encounter (366). Forgetting the sphere not only erases their memories, but makes the sphere disappear forever (362). Beth, Harry, and Norman successfully use their imaginations to alter reality for the entire human race.

On the other hand, a less commendable aspect to this final effort haunts the novel's ending. In willing themselves to forget the existence of the sphere forever, Beth, Harry, and Norman have enacted the supreme repression. Doing consciously what the human personality does unconsciously, the three heroes force themselves to forget an aspect of their lives. They do this because they fear the sphere. They nearly failed to control it, and they do not want to deal with it ever again. Readers are left to wonder if by so doing they have really rid the surface world of potential danger. Perhaps they have merely imprisoned a supreme power, which when unleashed once again in the future, will explode with an even stronger rage.

NOTE

1. As evidence of the pervasiveness of this theme, included here are a few publications that deal with the idea of responsibility in society. ABC news broadcast a national special entitled "Blame Game: A Nation of Victims?" on October 26, 1994. *The Abuse Excuse* by Alan Dershowitz drew much attention. In its August 15, 1994 issue, *Newsweek* asked, "Is redemption possible for this juvenile murderer or must he claim a share of his family's terrible legacy?" Other articles suggested that infidelity may be in our genes (*Time*, August 15, 1994), that the United States is a nation of crybabies (*Psychology Today*, October 1993), and that officials in Washington, D.C., live in a world where nobody gets blamed for their mistakes (*U.S. News and World Report*, October 10, 1994).

8

Congo
(1980)

With *Congo*, Michael Crichton departed from his usual urban or scientific settings. Here he plunged his cast of characters into the teeming, mysterious world of the African rain forest. In this story, Crichton's American heroes race a Japanese-European consortium into the heart of the jungle to locate lost diamond mines. Supported by both native porters and sophisticated, satellite-linked technology, the group soon discovers that the expected dangers of the Congo—cannibals, leeches, and wild animals—present the least of their worries. Soon they learn that earlier explorers have been killed mysteriously. Their camps have been destroyed and their skulls crushed with inhuman force. Attempts to locate the lost treasure soon take second place to identifying and surviving this horrifying murderous power.

Crichton's thrilling novel quickly became a best-seller. The film rights to the story sold even before a screenplay had been drafted. The novel, however, took a long time to appear as a film, because Crichton found he simply could not adapt it. "I discovered I was more interested in the periphery of the story than in the center" (Sauter, 22). However, a film version of *Congo* was released in 1995—complete with special effects wizard Stan Winston (creator of the dinosaur effects for the film *Jurassic Park*) designing the murderous guardian gorillas.

Like many of Crichton's other novels, *Congo* is strongly influenced by the history of a particular type of fiction. The generic conventions of the adventure story helped shape the development of plot, character, and theme. Crichton's innovative placement of a female scientist at the head of the exploration team, however, changes the all-male alliances that usually populate such fiction, and suggests the feminist critical reading that follows.

GENERIC CONVENTIONS

According to Michael Crichton, *Congo* is "basically a nineteenth century adventure story" (Sauter, 22). The adventure story, with its action-filled plot and enduring heroes, has entertained people for centuries. Ancient epics such as *The Iliad*, *The Odyssey*, and the medieval tales of King Arthur remain well known. Novels such as *The Last of the Mohicans* and *White Fang*, and more recently films such as *Raiders of the Lost Ark* and *Star Wars*, all thrilled their audiences in similar ways. Each features a "hero accomplishing some important and moral mission" (Cawelti, 39). The heroes overcome obstacles presented by their evil adversaries and the harsh environment. Adventure stories provide an exciting fantasy as the hero defeats every possible threat, even death.

While *Congo* certainly owes a debt to the body of adventure literature that preceded it (see Chapter 2), in particular it echoes one immensely popular novel. *King Solomon's Mines*, by Sir Henry Rider Haggard, was published in 1885. Haggard himself found inspiration in the works of Robert Louis Stevenson, particularly *Treasure Island*. *King Solomon's Mines* has influenced a large body of literature since its publication. Most notable is Joseph Conrad's classic exploration of imperialism, self-discovery, and destruction, *Heart of Darkness* (1899), which also affected the development of Crichton's *Congo*.

To the adventure story framework, Crichton added the flavor of science fiction by weaving high technology into his story. This updated it and distracted the reader from "the basic preposterousness" of the adventure tale. Ultimately, Crichton believed "the whole thing . . . became . . . too great a literary stretch" (Sauter, 22) to be effective. Critics generally agreed, saying the novel's story disappeared amid lectures about geography and how to teach gorillas human sign language. Had he stayed with a more pure adventure format (as he did with *The Great Train Robbery*), *Congo* might have achieved greater success. Nonetheless, *Congo* remains strongly linked to its adventure story heritage, and, as

the next sections show, its plot, characters, and themes have been extensively influenced by that history.

PLOT DEVELOPMENT

The adventure story's success comes chiefly from plot. Episodic plotting, which features the constant introduction of new obstacles that the
protagonists (or heroes) must overcome to achieve their goal, can become
difficult for an author to handle in a believable fashion. A catalogue of
details typical of adventure stories includes perils with which most readers are familiar. A treasure map, a perilous quest, and a journey through
an extreme climate begin the adventure. Murderous natives, earlier explorers who have mysteriously disappeared, threatening wild animals,
and an ancient city all challenge the heroes. When they do find the long
lost treasure, burial alive and the loss of the jewels still threaten them.
Each episode must build on the others, presenting believable dangers.
Each must also continually develop more difficult and horrible situations. As the odds grow continually worse, the characters must achieve
at greater physical and intellectual levels to survive. To develop a compelling plot, authors introduce strong antagonists—people who oppose
the heroes' actions. Also, they set the adventure in a harsh and isolated
environment. Authors also increase the odds against the heroes even
further by stripping them of their civilized crutches. Weapons, communications, shelter, and medicines are destroyed as the heroes pursue their
quest. Their isolation prevents them from seeking help. Ultimately, the
heroes must depend more and more on their own strengths to survive.

Congo shares all of these traditional plot characteristics, spiced up with
some late-twentieth-century technology. The book opens with Karen
Ross of ERTS (Earth Resources Technology Services, Inc.) establishing a
satellite video link between her command center in Houston, Texas, and
the field team located in the Congo area of Africa. To her horror, the
panning of the automated video camera reveals the Congo camp destroyed and the scientists murdered, their heads crushed. The film captures a fleeting glimpse of a large gray animal moving away from the
scene.

Despite this devastation, ERTS's interest in the Congo is compelling
enough for them to send a second team, headed by Ross. This group
also includes an experienced field guide, a scientist who specializes in
communicating with gorillas, and his domesticated gorilla, who "speaks"

through sign language. The group embarks on a quest for lost diamond mines which will yield fabulous wealth. These mines are the world's only known source for type IIb boron-coated diamonds, which will make computers calculate faster than the speed of light. Such computers will bring military supremacy to whoever develops them. Therefore, the owners of the diamonds can sell them for a fortune. The driving conflict of the plot develops as the ERTS team and a team from another company race to find the mines.

The next conflict arises as these teams encounter the natural world of the Congo. As the heroes plunge through the heart of Africa in search of their treasure, they must overcome ever-escalating crises. Extreme heat gives way to freezing mountain terrain. Cannibals rampage in protest over new government policies. Wild hippopotami attack humans who invade their territory. A solar flare disrupts satellite communications with the technology center in Houston. This robs them of the computer power needed to discover efficient routes and areas to dig. It also deprives them of communications. These "civilized" humans must learn to respect the power of the jungle world in order to survive there.

Adventure stories also feature the heroes in conflict with evil natives. While *Congo* does include a tribe of rampaging cannibals, the focus of evil in Africa lies with the gray gorillas, guardians of the diamond mines of Zinj. This focus is highlighted as the explorers enter the jungle and encounter a survivor of the earlier expedition. His distraught condition terrifies them. Indirectly, the evil the heroes face comes from the ancient inhabitants of Zinj, who bred and trained these gorillas to shatter the skulls of strangers who approached the city. As the scientist, Peter Elliot, explains to the others, the gorillas are "as smart as a human being" and vicious. "They will continue their attacks until they succeed in killing us all" (252). Despite their deadliness, these antagonists remain strangely hard for readers to hate. As trained animals, they can hardly be held responsible for what they do. They are, in fact, admirable for their undaunted attempts to fulfill their mission. The truly guilty parties appear only by proxy. The inhabitants of Zinj are long dead, but their lethal legacy of specially bred and trained gorillas lives on.

These guardian gorillas efficiently destroy any humans who come too near to the diamond mines they guard. Delayed by circumstances in the jungle, the ERTS team despairs of beating the other team to the mines. When they arrive, however, they find the other team murdered, their camp destroyed. The information they gather from examining the destruction helps them prepare for their own battle with the gorillas. That night, the gorillas' first attack proves to the humans that, despite their complex weaponry, they cannot withstand many encounters with the beasts. It also reveals that the gorillas communicate with some form of verbal language—a skill previously unknown in animals. In order to survive, the scientists must use their own trained gorilla to learn and translate the guardians' language so they can call them off the attack. When that works, the team rushes to the mines.

The climax and resolution of the conflict also follow adventure story tradition. As in Haggard's novel, the heroes find the lost mines, but a series of mishaps forces them to flee without their treasure. Only the savvy jungle guide has the sense to fill his pockets with diamonds as he runs. Crichton's heroes must flee from a volcanic eruption that collapses the mines and from the dangers of the jungle. At first they attempt to escape on foot, but soon cannibals trap them inside the cargo plane flown in by the other company's team. The eruption destroys their satellite link so they cannot call for help. Their ammunition will not last. When technology fails to save them, they find a rather familiar escape route. A hot air balloon—just like the ones in such adventures as Verne's *Around the World in Eighty Days* and Baum's *The Wonderful Wizard of Oz* (1900)—whisks them away to safety.

CHARACTER DEVELOPMENT

The conventions of adventure fiction also shape the development of character in *Congo*. Adventure story characters generally fall into easily identifiable categories. The most developed of these are the Westernized heroes who must survive the jungle and the friendly natives who help them.

Heroes in adventure tales generally fall into two groups, both of which are represented in *Congo*. First is the superhero, a person of exceptional knowledge and capabilities who leads the others through their adventure. Captain Munro stands out among Crichton's characters as this sort of hero. Mysterious and dangerous, Munro is known as a gun-runner and soldier-for-hire. He is the most expensive bush guide available, but also the best. However, his self-centered motives are guided by an amazing common sense. When the computer's suggested routes through the jungle are all too slow, Munro merely plots a course over it. He flies the team as far as he can, then parachutes them all into the wilderness. This cuts days from their schedule. He is unimpressed by, and therefore not reliant on, the advanced technology the scientists bring. Later, when the computers become useless, he alone remains functional. He recognizes and appreciates the true nature of individuals and of the jungle world and does not try to impress his own expectations upon others. Though he is an expert field guide, he possesses a healthy respect for the jungle (159). Though he knows little about primate research, he communicates well with Amy, a domesticated gorilla who travels with them. He respects her personality, both as a gorilla and as a female (152). He is the first person to figure out the secrets of Zinj's murderous gorillas because he does not try to impose his own values on the ancient ruins. This adaptability keeps him and his companions alive through one disaster after another.

The other main characters, Dr. Karen Ross and Dr. Peter Elliot, fall into the second category of hero. They are realistic, flawed people with whom readers can easily identify. At first, Karen Ross seems superhuman. She is a math and computer prodigy. She earned a Ph.D. at age twenty-four and now directs a research team for Earth Resources Technology Service. She seems exceptionally brave, demanding to lead a new field team into the Congo after the first expedition is destroyed. Her responses to situations throughout the plot, however, reveal her less admirable characteristics. Ross seeks leadership because the authority thrills her (27). Time after time she endangers her own life and the others' in pursuit of her goal. After learning of an injured man in the jungle, she insists they abandon him because helping him will take too much time (167). When one of her own party dies, she mourns, but only about her project. "She seemed genuinely affected with human feeling . . . but she continued, 'The whole expedition is falling apart' " (225–226). Later, when even Munro insists they leave the jungle, she refuses (259). She conceals information about a coming volcanic eruption so that they will continue to help her. Ultimately, it is her desperate need to succeed that triggers the earthquake and, ironically, buries the diamond mines under half a mile of lava.

In contrast to Ross, Peter Elliot cares little about finding diamonds. Like his scientific counterpart, however, he pursues his own goal to prove his theories about animal intelligence. Elliot pretends to be boyish and shy, a typical academic, because he finds it useful. He is, however, intelligent and aware of almost everything that goes on around him, and unafraid to ask questions of Munro. Elliot rejoices in even the unpleasant aspects of his first experience in the African jungle because it is real, not just information from a book. When faced with a charging gorilla, Elliot wonders if he was foolish to believe everything he had read. He is thrilled, however, to realize that "these gorillas had behaved in exactly the textbook manner" (198). Unlike Munro and Ross, Elliot finds the life-threatening adventures genuinely horrifying. His fears make readers like him all the more. For example, after the parachute drop, which terrified him, he "felt extraordinarily fine . . . the next instant he fell over on rubber legs and promptly threw up" (142). He avoids engaging in combat with natives or wild animals, but when faced with a fight-or-die situation, Elliot comes through (308). Readers appreciate Elliot's sensitivity, for even though he has saved everyone's lives, he does not rejoice in murder.

The helpful natives who inhabit adventure stories are those who, through loyalty to the bush guide, assist the heroes on their adventure. *Congo* hosts a cast of such people, including humanitarian pygmies and the native porters. They provide little more than local color in the development of the novel, however. The notable exception is Amy, the seven-year-old mountain gorilla. She has lived for six years with Peter Elliot, learning to communicate with American Sign Language (ASL). Crichton's development of Amy as a character led one critic to claim that *Congo* was "literarily vapid and scientifically more anthropomorphic than 'Dumbo' " (Hayes, 13), but that judgment seems somewhat harsh. Amy, like many animals, possesses an intuitive sense about people. She adores Elliot, who raised her, and she enjoys Munro, who simply treats her like a gorilla. But she dislikes Ross, who treats her like a retarded child. In the jungle, she sticks close to the humans. She warns them that the land near Zinj is a bad place where people die. This evaluation is confirmed when Munro and Elliot find human bones shattered on the ground.

Amy's intuition and ability to communicate save the humans' lives on several occasions. When Elliot falls into a group of guardian gorillas, she charges into the field, hollering with rage, and cradles him like an infant (265). Mystified, the gorillas leave quietly, honoring the life of a supposedly helpless being. Later, her ability to understand both humans and animals gives Amy alone the knowledge that saves the explorers from the murderous gorillas. Though she fears them, Amy learns to understand their language. Her ability to translate it into sign language for Elliot and Munro provides them with their only chance at defense. Amy is indeed the noble savage.

THEMATIC ISSUES

Nineteenth-century adventure stories typically focused on the clash between European cultures and other "primitive" societies. The imperialism of Victorian England had dominated much of the world for decades. Europeans in general genuinely felt driven to bring "civilization" to the "savages" of Africa, India, and Asia. A similar theme developed in American adventure novels. There, inhabitants of the eastern states pushed westward and encountered the "primitives" of Indian tribes. However, in the best adventure stories, like the works of Haggard, good and evil did not divide clearly along cultural boundaries. Europeans and Africans shared both the blessings and the curses of morality. Though Haggard presented native Africans who act with unspeakable savagery and evil, he also created natives capable of great good. In some cases they were more noble and more capable of survival than the European characters. However, the difference between the cultures remained distinct and wide. Primitive natives and civilized Europeans shared very little in terms of their cultural experiences. They could not avoid shock when dealing with each other.

Crichton alters the typical adventure theme of the culture clash to fit the modern world. In the shrinking world of the twentieth century, such cultural distinctions are no longer as clear. Though vastly different in many ways, European and African nations have more in common now than they did 100 years ago. Some of the greatest dangers Munro's group faces are the very modern heat-seeking missiles and artillery shells of Zaire's army. Miniaturization and materials development have allowed the Westerners to carry much of their own culture into the jungle with them. They dine on rehydrated food and sleep in sealed shelters with air-conditioning units. They receive constant updates on weather and military movements through computer-satellite links, and fight off dangers with automatic laser-guided machine guns. The Westerners avoid natives rather than seeking them out. They prefer simply getting on their way toward the diamond mines.

Instead of devoting his novel to an examination of clashing human cultures, Crichton focuses on the differences between animals and humans. He points out that using the human/animal distinction as a gauge for intelligence is not always clear (32). Language use is the often cited proof that humans are more intelligent than "dumb" animals. But in *Congo*, Crichton defies that distinction. The novel reflects on "the endless possibilities and permutations of communication" (Hayes, 13) in a variety of ways. Armed with technology, humans communicate with each other from opposite sides of the world. But at least one human, Elliot, communicates with a gorilla, and she with him, through American Sign Language. When the explorers discover a species of gorilla that has developed a spoken language, Amy in turn translates this language into sign language for the humans to use. An animal, not a human, becomes the most able communicator, primarily because she lacks established prejudices about the intelligence and abilities of others.

To achieve full understanding of and communication with others, individuals must remain open-minded enough to use all available resources appropriately, as does Amy. The team's bush leader, Captain Munro, also achieves this. He honors pygmy and cannibal customs and languages when interacting with them. He treats Amy like the young female gorilla that she is. And he does not become overdependent on data transmitted via satellite from halfway around the world. To an extent, Elliot does this as well, primarily with the wild gorillas he encounters. But when faced with the new species, his prejudices take over: "We kept expecting the gorillas to behave in stupid, stereotyped ways but they never did" (257). Only Munro escapes this tendency. He decides that since men had trained them, the gorillas should be treated like men (257). This decision helps the team escape.

This connection of animals with humans is not merely a *Bambi*-inspired anthropomorphism—assigning human traits to animals—on Crichton's part. In fact, it extends beyond that. Crichton expresses an appreciation and respect that humans normally reserve only for other humans. His attitude grew from his own experience observing gorillas near Zaire. During his first sighting, Crichton reports that he was attacked by the silverback male (*Travels*, 260). Crichton stood his ground, as instructed, and the gorilla backed off. He later recreated this scene with Peter Elliot in *Congo*. The episode filled Crichton with a deep appreciation of these animals and their ways. "I had the distinct sense that we all understood one another" (*Travels*, 262–263). Later, remembering his trip, Crichton observed, "No other primates are like gorillas, they might as well be people" (Sauter, 24). The demand for respect, not cute behavior, makes these animals seem human to Crichton.

The unique value of animal intelligence even outstrips humans' use of science and technology. When he needs solid information regarding dangerous areas or seismic activity, Munro consults Amy instead of Ross and her computers. In this he differs from Ross and Elliot who, instead of using computers as an *aid* to human perceptions, tend to depend *entirely* on the machines (247). Here, Crichton dramatizes a contemporary social tendency that concerns him. "I'm enthusiastic about science, but there is a growing tendency toward scientism—unthinking acceptance of scientific ideas and a tendency to discount ideas that science can't address" (Fox, 38). In *Congo*, only a solar flare that renders the computers useless forces Ross and Elliot to turn to more natural sources of intelligence. Even then they do so with trepidation. "Elliot found it strange to think that his own brain was inadequate" (270). But an animal brain *is* adequate. From this situation they are saved by Amy's revelation "*Amy understand thing talk*" (271). When he cannot use his computers, Elliot finally appreciates Amy. After years of learning ASL from Peter, Amy now teaches Peter the essentials of the guardian gorilla language.

Though Crichton's theme strays far from the traditional themes of adventure fiction in its details, the message is essentially the same. Novels like Haggard's stress that a human's moral values should not be judged on the basis of racial or cultural history. Crichton's book similarly suggests that the value of a being's intelligence should not be judged simply on the basis of its humanity or its ability to use spoken language. There are aspects to animal intelligence that human science cannot understand. If we remain unreceptive to those resources—as the Congo explorers almost do—we may not survive.

A FEMINIST READING OF *CONGO*

Survival is an especially important issue for Karen Ross. As the young female leader of the expedition into the Congo, she has her personal and professional reputation on the line as well as her life. As explained in Chapter 4's overview of feminism, examination of Crichton's presentation of women reveals much about the ideas in his fiction. In *Congo*, as in *The Terminal Man*, Crichton uses a female character to illustrate what happens to women who desire power and control. The female characters even share nearly identical names: Dr. Janet Ross in *The Terminal Man* and Dr. Karen Ross in *Congo*. In this novel Crichton shows that traditional femininity is not an acceptable model for behavior. Yet at the same time, he suggests that women who enter the traditional masculine world are also doomed to failure.

Crichton's discussion clearly links the female gender with traditional, demeaning stereotypes of femininity. Such a stereotypic definition of femininity would rile many feminist readers, especially when the description refers to an adolescent mountain gorilla. Very few women would desire to develop the traits he describes as "distinctly feminine" (57). They are all linked to a narcissistic preoccupation with appearances. "She could be coy, she responded to flattery . . . loved make-up, and was very fussy about the color of the sweaters she wore in winter.... She was openly jealous of Elliot's girl friends" (57–58). The tone of the scene suggests that these traits genuinely define femininity for Crichton. Femininity, it seems, is not even human.

The male characters' views of Ross mirror Crichton's use of gender-based stereotypes. They continually assess Ross not according to her abilities, but according to her gender. Her boss, Travis, worries about sending her into the field. He does not care that her personality profile suggests that she will crush under pressure. He worries because she is young and female (25). Munro treats her similarly. In the Congo, as the group climbs a freezing mountain, Ross collapses, exhausted. The only way Munro can prod her into traveling further is by humiliating her with "Just like a woman" (188). All the characters in the book seem to agree about the undesirability of femininity.

No doubt as a result of such attitudes and her desire to be successful, Ross herself also disdains traditional femininity. She identifies herself instead with the logic of math and computers. Driven to avoid a feminine identity, Ross seems to have instead built a self-image grounded on competence. This "unfeminine" presentation, however, fails to earn her a more comfortable place in society. "She had a self-possession that most people found striking—even a little unsettling" (10). People dislike Ross because of her sound self-confidence and remarkable ability, traits interesting in a male but threatening in a female.

Crichton makes it clear that the lack of acceptance Ross has felt from other people has led to the development of many of her undesirable personality traits. "The years of isolation . . . had left her aloof and rather distant" (10). Ross has lost the ability to connect empathically to the people and environment around her. Thus she misses the potential for enjoyment in her life. As Elliot and the others thrill at the jungle's sense of freedom and adventure, she adjusts her computer. When Elliot suddenly finds her "beautiful and graceful," she "did not look back at him" (144). Her lack of connection goes even farther, making her seem occasionally heartless and cruel. She refuses to help an injured stranger, even when Munro explains that he will die without their help (167). Despite his pleas, her concerns remain her own. "If we go to that village, we blow the rest of the day" (167). Even when faced with the gory deaths of previous explorers, she remains cool and analytical (110, 225), almost inhuman. Ross resembles a cartoon of a human being, more like the computers she devotes her life to than the people she travels with.

Devoted only to her professional, logical, controllable life, Ross will do anything to achieve her established goal, in this case, locating lost diamond mines ahead of her competitors. The psychological evaluation done by her employers calls her "ruthless . . . domineering . . . intellectually arrogant . . . driven to succeed at any cost" (26). Ross does not think those traits are necessarily bad (305). They should help her become a successful field leader. As head of the Congo fieldwork, she has much at stake. With such intense pressure on her, as well as an awareness that she is responsible for *"billions of dollars"* (103), it is no wonder that her need to succeed provokes "dangerously illogical responses" (27). Ross, like the other female in the novel, Amy, will become aggressive when provoked. "And an attack by Amy was never amusing" (57–58).

Ross's only emotional moments come when she loses control over her situation. In the first instance, Ross suddenly finds that she cannot link her computer to the Houston control center and receive calculated odds for the group's parachute jump. "For the first time in her memory, Karen Ross wanted to cry" (137). Later, after the attack by the male mountain gorilla, Ross collapses in Elliot's arms, sobbing (198). "The shock of discovering that the natural world followed its own rules and was indifferent . . . represented a harsh psychic blow" (137) to Ross. She has been accustomed to coping with any situation through technology.

The tragedy of Karen Ross's situation, and of Crichton's depiction of women in *Congo*, is that Ross does not grow from her ordeals. She remains unchanged, stuck behind a wall of desperate confusion. As the expedition prepares to enter the mines, Ross's control center in Houston orders her via satellite to flee the area because of the coming volcanic eruption. But success is too important to her (288). Ross turns the computer off and does not tell the others about the danger. Her confidence and independence have strengthened. She nearly cried earlier when she couldn't contact Houston, but here she divorces herself completely from them. However, that confidence renders her remarkably dangerous. With the mountain rumbling above them, Ross sets twelve explosive charges inside the mines. She ignores Munro's warnings and suggestions that they seek advice from Houston. This sets off the earthquake and the volcanic eruption, and the group barely escapes alive. The city is buried, and the mines with it, under nearly half a mile of lava. Though Ross eventually becomes "aware of an ironic ending to her personal quest" (305), she never accepts full responsibility for her actions. She had been "beaten by the worst volcanic eruption in Africa in a decade. Who could blame her for what had happened? It wasn't her fault. She would prove that on her next expedition" (305). Her need to prove herself through further attempts at power and control will apparently continue to govern her life.

Many aspects of *Congo* seem to have come straight from Crichton's own life. Perhaps his depiction of Karen Ross does as well. Crichton talks about the anxiety he experienced as a traveler when faced with something he could not understand. Describing an ancient Mayan ruin he once visited, Crichton wrote: "It was almost intolerable to look at this vast complex and to admit that we didn't know about it. We *had* to know. It was too large for us not to know" (*Travels*, 188). Because he cannot know for certain, Crichton admits that he, and many historians, hypothesize. "The internal psychological pressure to make up a story . . . is powerful indeed" (*Travels*, 190). Perhaps Crichton does similar explaining about femininity, a vast complex that he, as a man, cannot experience, but can guess about from his own experience.

9

Jurassic Park
(1990)

Of the 20 million paperbacks in print by Michael Crichton, 42 percent of them—8.4 million—are *Jurassic Park* (Pener). The popularity of Crichton's 1988 novel soared with the phenomenal success of Steven Speilberg's 1993 film version, which quickly rose to the status of all-time top grossing motion picture.[1] *Jurassic Park* tells the tale of wealthy entrepreneur John Hammond, whose staff has succeeded in cloning dinosaurs. He now intends to open a wildlife park on an island to showcase them. His investors worry, however, about the safety of the system. They insist that a team of independent experts examine and approve of the facilities before they provide more capital. Paleontologists Alan Grant and Ellie Sattler, mathematician Ian Malcolm, attorney Donald Gennaro, and computer designer Dennis Nedry visit the island. There they find that the investors' worries are indeed well founded.

This chapter looks at five aspects of Crichton's most popular novel. Plot construction makes this a fast-paced and suspenseful novel. Character development presents a variety of perspectives on the park. Crichton employs major generic conventions established in the science fiction and gothic heritage. The cultural and social context of the novel develops the major themes. Finally, the critical reading of this novel suggests how a Marxist literary critic might view *Jurassic Park*.

PLOT DEVELOPMENT

Jurassic Park's plot makes it a novel readers find impossible to put down. In its numerous episodes, relation of cause and effect, suspense, and conflict, the novel presents a series of events that continually engage our interest anew.

Plots developed on the episodic pattern so familiar to popular literature present authors with a major problem. How does an author generate a series of harrowing situations for the main characters without creating a ridiculously unrealistic story line? Crichton avoids this potential pitfall by rotating the focus of his chapters among the main characters, who spend much of the book separated from each other. This rotation allows Crichton to generate frequent excitement without unrealistically having the same group encounter a climax in each chapter. The parade of short, exciting episodes becomes all the more thrilling because Crichton constructs them believably.

Crichton further produces a gripping plot by carefully constructing cause and effect. His straightforward, almost cinematic presentation clearly indicates how one mishap or judgment in error leads to another. Mathematician Ian Malcolm's constant lecturing on chaos theory reinforces this structure. Even the unpredictable is predicted, in fact *caused*, by the attempts to control the environment at the park. Malcolm knows that humans cannot control life's inherent unpredictability. Therefore, he foresees the failure of the systems that control the island even before they are built. Malcolm's statements to the others set the stage for the book's events. The disasters build one upon the other as parts of Malcolm's chaos theory.

In addition to containing tightly woven events, the plot's structure helps build suspense, most notably in the opening of the book. Crichton presents several episodes that seem only loosely connected to the main plot. But they are essential to developing a suspenseful grip on the reader through dramatic irony. This is a situation in which a reader knows more than the central character. The book opens with vivid depictions of strange lizard-like creatures mauling children. These episodes firmly establish our awareness of the animals' horrible destructive potential and create suspense as we await the next attack on an innocent victim. Readers remember these detached episodes as they encounter Jurassic Park for the first time. The bloody bodies contrast strongly with the peaceful sight of a giant apatosaur gently trumpeting in the distance. Though heroes Alan Grant and Ellie Sattler stand entranced, we know that violence threatens everyone on the island. The dramatic irony increases our tension and keeps us turning pages in suspense.

Development of suspense also requires readers' interest in the conflicts that shape the plot. In *Jurassic Park*, two central conflicts create the disasters from which our heroes must escape. First is the conflict of human beings versus the natural order, one seen many times throughout the book. The most important example occurs when John Hammond and his bioengineering staff genetically engineer live dinosaurs. The genetic engineers, led by Dr. Henry Wu, attempt to alter the natural behaviors of these animals. For instance, they create only females so that the animals cannot reproduce. They make the dinosaurs dependent on lysine, so that if an animal leaves the boundaries of the park, it will die. Wu and Hammond fail to see the dinosaurs as wild creatures that will follow their instincts to reproduce, migrate, and survive. Instead they view the dinosaurs as amusements that can be controlled by fencing and hidden cameras. Nature, however, even when reconstructed by humans, does not so easily submit to human control. Eventually the dinosaurs' instincts overcome every containment. Then the humans must flee the unleashed power of the carnivorous giants they constructed.

The second major conflict of *Jurassic Park* involves the individual versus society. This is most prominent when an individual's self-interest conflicts with consideration for others. Each time someone chooses self-interest over the welfare of others, the situation at Jurassic Park becomes worse. Perhaps the most striking example of this conflict is seen in John Hammond's attempts to convince his investors that the park is safe. In a display of complete confidence, Hammond brings his small grandchildren to the island, placing them in terrible danger. Others make similar mistakes. Henry Wu brings the dinosaurs to life but remains ignorant of their abilities to escape, hunt, and reproduce. When computer programmer Dennis Nedry shuts down the security systems to steal materials from the labs, he lets loose the dinosaurs which kill him and others. Ed Regis abandons the children in the face of a tyrannosaurus attack—twice. This prevents their return to the control rooms, where only they can save the others.

However, when individuals choose to risk their own self-interest for the good of others, ultimately they also benefit. Alan Grant gives up his chance to escape the roaming dinosaurs when he opts to help the children. Ultimately this saves not only his own life, but the lives of all the survivors. Only the children can turn on the park's computerized power and security systems. Ellie Sattler volunteers to distract the velociraptors so that others can run between buildings and restore power to the computers. This not only helps the children's efforts, but grants Ellie the most exhilarating self-fulfillment of her life. Donald Gennaro's decision to risk his own life when rescuing others teaches him the relative valuelessness of money and prestige.

CHARACTER DEVELOPMENT

In adventure and science fiction, plot development traditionally overshadows the development of character. Crichton's own work follows this pattern. Often his characters seem stereotypic, or two-dimensional entities created primarily for the purpose of enduring events. The characters of *Jurassic Park* are essentially static because they do not grow significantly. However, together they represent a variety of approaches to the themes that the plot develops. The protagonists—the lead characters who engage readers' sympathy—are all people who respect the uncontrollable powers of nature. Though the book has been accused by critics and scientists alike of "bashing" science, *Jurassic Park* presents most people interested in the sciences as unequivocal heroes. The paleontologists Grant and Sattler are consistently motivated by a dedication to their field. When they do pursue money, they do so only to fund their continuing studies of Montana fossils. When they discover the live dinosaurs, they care for them as miraculous sources of information. They never think of them as money-makers. Grant cannot contain his delight at discovering the truth about dinosaur habits, even when it proves his own theories incorrect. Sattler's quick application of paleobotany saves a dying stegosaurus. When trouble strikes, they assess the realities of any situation and react sensibly, selflessly, and successfully.

Like the paleontologists, Ian Malcolm responds to situations from a dedication to his own specialty, chaos theory. His constant predictions of disaster strike many of the characters as irrational pessimism. But in the end the others respect the accuracy of his insights. Though he seems very negative, he ultimately proves brave and generous. He continually tries to make his friends understand more about the uncontrollable nature of the world in which they live.

Tim Murphy, though only eleven years old, takes learning as seriously as his adult friends. Given the limits of time and education, Tim knows paleontology as well as Alan Grant. And even within those limits, Tim knows more about computers than anyone left alive at the end of the book. Tim ultimately proves more successful than any of the heroic adults because he has skills in many areas. Like Grant, he knows enough paleontology to survive the wilds of the park. Like Malcolm, Tim can engage in abstract thinking well enough to run an unfamiliar computer system. Though Tim's life has been full of rejection, he achieves a sense of self-worth through this disaster.

Donald Gennaro, attorney for Jurassic Park's financial backers, represents the most "average" personality among the characters. Like many of us, he is a basically good person, interested primarily in survival. Initially he wants only to succeed in his profession and protect his clients. But as Jurassic Park presents him with horrors greater than displeasing his boss, Gennaro consistently rises to the challenges. This seems only right, however, since he helped create this disaster. As Grant says, "You sold investors on an undertaking you didn't fully understand.... You did not check on the activities of a man whom you knew from experience to be a liar, and you permitted that man to screw around with the most dangerous technology in human history" (372). When challenged, Gennaro does see the truth and acts appropriately.

The antagonists—the characters who oppose the protagonists—in *Jurassic Park* present an even wider array of perspectives and personalities. But they all share one trait. They do not appreciate the true nature of things. Instead, they are preoccupied with the desire for self-gratification, largely through wealth and prestige. The creator of the park, John Hammond, is the most complex character in Crichton's novel. To the others he seems a harmless old man. "John Hammond's about as sinister as Walt Disney" in the eyes of Alan Grant (42). He speaks with "irritating, cheery persistence" (46). In keeping with this image, Hammond deludes himself into thinking that the Jurassic Park project is a noble effort to benefit the world's children. "The children of the world love dinosaurs, and the children are going to delight . . . in this place. Their little faces will shine with the joy of finally seeing these wonderful animals" (199). However, without any understanding of his self-contradiction, Hammond also admits his intent to make a lot of money. "Would you make products to help mankind fight illness and disease? Dear me, no. That's a terrible idea. A very poor use of new technology," he argues. Government regulations and price controls make "helping mankind a very risky business. Personally, I would *never* help mankind" (200). His inability to understand the implications of his thoughts and actions make Hammond an extremely dangerous man. Even Henry Wu is bothered by Hammond's tendency to evade issues (198). Crichton shows this when Hammond's grandchildren get lost in the park. Hammond responds with alarming detachment, eating ice cream while others search for them (228). Later, as the park crumbles around him, with all but a handful of people dead, Hammond fails to understand the lesson of his experience. "Say what they would, he knew that his park had promise" (381). Only a terrible fright caused by his grandchildren prevents him from trying again.

Dennis Nedry, the computer consultant who designed all the systems that run Jurassic Park, shares with Hammond the responsibility for the disaster that occurs there. However, unlike Hammond, Nedry is consciously unscrupulous. He knowingly places the park in danger so that he can steal embryos to sell to a rival company. Crichton combines Nedry's wickedness with revolting physical characteristics to create a cartoon of evil that readers love to hate. He is messy and overweight, his hands sticky from the candy he has eaten (76). His pride in outsmarting everyone else through expertise with computers eventually leads to his death. However, Nedry's system is not complex enough to prevent a bright eleven-year-old from restoring it.

Dr. Henry Wu, the genetic engineer who brings the dinosaurs to life, also seeks self-gratification through professional expertise. He has little concern for how his actions affect other lives. Wu doesn't know much about dinosaur behavior, and cannot even remember exactly what species he has created (107). He constructs plans to modify the creatures, not to make them more realistic or more healthy, but to match twentieth-century popular perceptions of the ancient animals (121–122). His pride even allows him to twist the perception of his errors into triumphs. Despite all his careful efforts, the dinosaurs begin to breed. "And though Wu would never admit it, the discovery that the dinosaurs were breeding represented a tremendous validation of his work" (334). Concerned primarily with publishing his work and enjoying the fame that will follow, Wu never appreciates the independent power of the life he has created, not even when it eats him alive.

The final important antagonist in *Jurassic Park* also fails to appreciate anything that occurs around her. She focuses entirely on self-gratification even when it endangers herself. Lex Murphy, Hammond's granddaughter and Tim's younger sister, constantly annoys and endangers everyone around her. Even the knowledge that Lex is anxious about her parents' divorce and misses her father dreadfully does not make readers sympathetic to her. She consistently proves herself useless (185), inactive

(208), weak (233), cruel (237, 274, 282), and a hindrance to others (265, 341). Although Lex is not responsible for the collapse of Jurassic Park, she is clearly a young version of her grandfather. Perhaps she is a future disaster waiting to happen.

GENERIC CONVENTIONS

As discussed in Chapter 2, Crichton consciously develops his work from the literary heritage of his chosen genre. *Jurassic Park* draws primarily on gothic and science fiction traditions. It also has similarities to classics of horror cinema. The novel closely resembles *Frankenstein*. Mary Shelley's classic work was the first novel to blend the horror and emotional intensity of gothic with the detail and presumed rationality of science. *Jurassic Park* follows in this classic novel's footsteps. Most gothic fiction focuses on the return of something dead or at least buried (for instance, Frankenstein's monster, vampires, werewolves, ghosts, dinosaurs). Often a long-hidden supernatural being brings complete disaster by revealing the true nature of itself and of the people with whom it comes in contact. Ironically, the *supernatural* being often proves more *natural*—or true to itself—than the other characters. In *Jurassic Park*, for example, the existence of the dinosaurs is engineered by misguided men enslaved by the desire or need for wealth. However, the dinosaurs turn out to be creatures with personalities and wills of their own. As in *Frankenstein*, the human scientists try to create life, but fail to prepare adequately for their success. Though living creatures are naturally willful and independent, the scientists expect to create easily controllable automatons. When the scientists do succeed in creating life, disaster strikes because of their failure to acknowledge the creatures' uncontrollable instincts.

Science fiction delivers similar messages about scientists who disrupt the realm of nature. But it also adds other important conventions. *Jurassic Park*, like classic science fiction, taps into popular fears by relying on a realistic depiction of contemporary science. "All great science fiction must be science first and fiction second. Even more, it must tap into the reigning scientific paradigm of its era. For Mary Shelley's *Frankenstein*, that paradigm was electricity. . . . For *Godzilla*, it was radioactivity and the Bomb. For *Jurassic Park*, it is biotechnology" (Begley, 57). And that paradigm, or theme, must be depicted with solid believability, for that is the "hidden persuader" (Begley, 57) of all science fiction.

Crichton's novel does not suggest that science itself is wicked. But it does point out that poor judgment by scientists has created "worrisome trends in a dramatic, potentially harmful, but correctable enterprise" (Marcus, 5). The scientists depicted in science fiction often are not evil, but clearly have "more skill than wisdom" (Skow, "Dino DNA"). In H. G. Wells's *The Island of Dr. Moreau*, the scientist pieces together new creatures from men and animals. Similarly, the Jurassic Park developers piece together dinosaurs from ancient and modern DNA. These are stunning feats of technical expertise, but are they good ideas? Once the technological challenge is met, the scientists are faced with responsibilities toward their creations. Here they fail. *Jurassic Park* explores "the doom that humankind faces if scientists are not diverted from their immoral and calamitous path" (Skolnick, 1252). Despite their strongest efforts, they cannot control nature. "It is man's utter incapacity to change nature that he [Crichton] finds so horrifyingly exciting, and that is the real thrill of *Jurassic Park*" (Place, 9).

Popular film has also influenced the presentation of *Jurassic Park*. *King Kong* and *Godzilla* typify movies that depict an ancient beast set loose in the modern world. The film version of Arthur Conan Doyle's *The Lost World* shows modern people who return to an ancient world. *The Birds, Jaws*, and other monster movies show animals attacking humans. And *The Blob* and *War of the Worlds* show the escalating power of unfamiliar creatures and the dangers they bring to humans. Crichton's childhood love of film and his professional success with film adaptations of his books no doubt influenced *Jurassic Park*.

CULTURAL AND SOCIAL CONTEXT AS DEVELOPED IN THEMATIC ISSUES

Like most successful science fiction, *Jurassic Park* focuses on contemporary attitudes toward science, featuring two related themes that hinge on contemporary debates. First, from attempts to save the spotted owl to surrogate motherhood to genetically engineered tomatoes, people in the late twentieth century worry about humans' ability and right to manipulate nature. True, we can control nature in little ways, like wearing glasses, building houses, and developing antibiotics. But in this novel, Crichton clearly suggests that we cannot completely control nature and are unwise to even attempt it.

Society has worried about science's limits for hundreds of years. But the awesome power of bioengineering presents more dangerous possibilities than ever before. Countless science fiction tales have shown that humans cannot control nature. What may look like control is really a match of our ideas and nature. *Frankenstein, The Island of Doctor Moreau,* Stephen King's *The Stand,* and even Crichton's own classic, *The Andromeda Strain,* all illustrate the futility of such attempts. According to Crichton, humans enter terrifying waters with bioengineering.

> You can make everything from new kinds of plastics to new kinds of pesticides to new kinds of perfumes to new kinds of medicines to new kinds of fish and game, new kinds of pets, new kinds of pet foods. Eventually you may be able to make computers with it. You may be able to make electronic organisms with it, so the notion of controlling this technology in any coherent way is kind of impossible. (*"Jurassic Park," Future Watch*)

If we cannot control the technology, what disaster might we bring upon ourselves? That is the cultural concern that shapes this story.

Throughout the novel, Ian Malcolm warns that humanity's prideful attempts to control nature will bring horrors upon ourselves. Identified as "the novel's intellectual and philosophical center" (Gould, 53), Malcolm suggests that humans can avoid danger only if they admit they cannot control nature. Because he believes nature is complex, Malcolm encourages the researchers to "understand what we don't understand" (91). He believes that our desire for control fosters an illusion of control. That illusion in turn justifies or motivates many of our actions. People desire to control nature, he argues, but they cannot ever succeed (351). We have the power to save ourselves, but we choose not to.

John Hammond and his staff routinely dismiss Malcolm's important message. That brings the crushing horror of the book. "Neither vast amounts of money nor the most sophisticated technologies can withstand the superior forces of nature" (Uhlir, 96) when humans feel only callous disregard for that power. In turn, humans have little significance to nature. They are just another animal on the plain to be hunted and devoured. Ultimately, nature is "hell-bent on obliterating man as she obliterates every lesser species," but "man is exclusively to blame for the ensuing hell" (Place, 8, 9). Humans can control neither the nature that already exists around us nor the nature of the creatures we create. Until we learn that, we contribute to our own demise with every step toward "progress."

The second major cultural theme of *Jurassic Park* develops from the first. Human weakness prevents the best use of technological power. Therefore new technology has dangerous potential for all humans. It follows, then, that the scientific research that develops technological power is too important to be left only to specialists. Some people fear that scientists will do anything just because it is possible, regardless of whether or not it is moral.

> *Jurassic Park*'s vision of hubristic scientists determined to shape the future, damn the consequences, recalls the physicists of the Manhattan Project. When they set off the Trinity test in Alamogordo, New Mexico, in 1945, they were not sure that the atomic bomb would not ignite the planet's entire atmosphere, consuming Earth in a world-ending holocaust. They did it anyway. (Begley, 61)

People in technology-developing countries want to know "whether there's anything to fear or whether anybody is keeping an eye on this stuff" (Hamilton, 34). Crichton's book calls for more public awareness of scientific research. People should control the direction in which such development will go. Crichton has said: "Just as war is too important to leave to the generals, science is too important to leave to scientists. Everyone needs to be attentive" (Begley, 61). One critic has even called the novel "a morality play on the relationship of the human race to science, technology, and nature" (Uhlir, 94).

However, many individuals in the scientific community view public disclosure and involvement as the potential end to development. They fear that people without expertise could ruin the future of experimentation. Therefore, they view any attempts at reform as attacks on science. Crichton's themes have led many readers and critics to claim that *Jurassic Park* engages in "science-bashing" the way some critics claim that *Rising Sun* bashes Japan. Given the novel's "pervasive 'anti-science' tone . . . some scientists are undoubtedly also feeling scared" (Marcus, 5).

In response to what they perceived as attacks by the novel itself, many members of the American scientific community attempted to discredit it. They claimed that Crichton inaccurately represented the developing technology and dismissed *Jurassic Park* as an invalid statement because the technological powers represented—cloning dinosaurs—are not accurate. For instance, because "no dinosaur-age arthropod has yet been found with blood in its stomach," the book has been called farfetched (Skolnick, 1252). The *Journal of the American Medical Association* issued the strongest statement:

> Science indeed may be in danger of extinction, but not because it no longer fits the world. Science is under increasing attack from the left and from the right, from "New Agers," promoters of quackery, creationists, flat-earthers, animal rights terrorists, and many others whose religious, philosophical, or political views do not hold up under the light of science. Crichton's monster tale should appeal to these enemies of science better than any Frankenstein incarnation ever did. (Skolnick, 1253)

Such critics claim that current government regulations adequately monitor biotechnology's growth. They further argue that it only benefits science and society if scientists seek profit from their research.

In contrast to these harsh judgments are equally strong statements of praise for the accuracy of Crichton's work. "Without the usual mad scientists or mutations caused by radiation accidents, Dr. Crichton's tale is grounded in the very latest advances in human knowledge . . . Dr. Crichton is adept at making every one of those ingredients comprehensible, often beguiling, frequently exciting" (Jennings, 14). Even famous naturalist Stephen Jay Gould calls Crichton's novel "the best possible scenario for making dinosaurs" (53). This resulted from Crichton's research. Before he wrote the book, Crichton asked an MIT specialist about it. "And he said, 'Oh, well, yeah, that could probably be done one day,' which I found very encouraging" ("Real Jurassic Park"). He found out that biologists have retrieved DNA from insects over 130 million years old, and from other extinct animals and plants (Begley, 58). He met with the Smithsonian Institution's Jack Horner, who has attempted to locate DNA in the ancient marrow of a tyrannosaurus rex. Crichton modeled Dr. Alan Grant on Horner. The rapid reproduction of the millions of links of DNA using computer technology that takes place in the novel mimics the real life polymerase chain reaction. Though no one has recreated an extinct life form from DNA, Mark Norrell of the American Museum of Natural History thinks "it'll be done very shortly. And that's not really an issue if it can be done; it's when it will be done" ("Could *Jurassic Park* Become a Reality?").

Thus, it seems difficult to label *Jurassic Park* science-bashing. In many cases, criticism of a particular practice is not a "bashing" of the endeavor in general. Instead it is a concern with abuse in an otherwise noble practice. Thus with *Jurassic Park*. Crichton acknowledges that he sees scientific advancements as "mixed blessings. Even the most exhilarating single moment of twentieth-century technology—landing a man on the moon—is now perceived for what it was, the first giant step in the systematic militarization of space" (*Electronic Life*, 4). His depiction of science "should not be dismissed simply as 'anti-science' any more than a movie critic's negative review should be regarded as anti-film" (Marcus, 5).

Many critics hope that the vast popularity of *Jurassic Park* will "stimulate interest in a wider conversation on the wisdom, ethics and control of genetic engineering, a subject that has received scant public attention, to our peril, in the last 15 years" (Fox, 38). Arthur Caplan of the Center for Biomedical Ethics admits that "people are worried about situations in which technological capacity outstrips our moral ability to grapple with it . . . about manipulating nature in ways that they don't feel they really understand" ("Could We"). Crichton hopes that "public involvement in medical research . . . will be greater now than it was, which may turn out to be a very good thing" (Crichton, "Heart Transplants," 34). However, defensive, angry, more secretive behavior toward an ever more watchful public could lead to an even greater rift between science and the public. "If biotech blows it with *Jurassic Park*, it won't be the first PR flub. Again and again, the nearly two-decade-old business has responded to controversy with: 'Trust us, we're scientists.' . . . Biotech may be in for a rude awakening" (Hamilton, 34).

A MARXIST READING OF *JURASSIC PARK*

This concern with the power of scientists motivated by greed instead of by the nobility of their profession suggests a Marxist reading of *Jurassic Park*. As explained in Chapter 5, a Marxist interpretation of a literary work considers it in terms of its larger socioeconomic context. Crichton's novel presents an ideal situation for a Marxist reading because it depicts a small but complete capitalistic society on Isla Nublar. Like many potentially perfect societies, this one is essentially cut off from the real world. It could have taken any social or governmental form the inhabitants wanted. In this case, capitalism governs. Everything on the island is dominated by the pursuit of wealth. The novel presents a perfect opportunity to analyze this social form—and shows it ending in total destruction.

At the center of all the events in *Jurassic Park* lies Isla Nublar, a purely capitalistic society where everything is based on economic motivation. Ethical or environmental considerations have no place. The island's owner/governor, Hammond, admits that his "intent was to use the newly emerging technology of genetic engineering to make money. A lot of money" (200). Though their areas of expertise differ, the members of his staff also labor only as a means to personal wealth. Attorney Donald Gennaro is a perfect example. He loses sight of his assignment—to determine the island's safety—when he sees his first dinosaur. Instead, he can only think, "We are going to make a fortune on this place. A *fortune*" (79). Crichton acknowledges that his novel mirrors real life. In reality, the most talented people, and therefore the greatest technological advancements, go to places like the fictional Isla Nublar where capitalism dominates. "Technology goes wherever there's a use for it, wherever there's a financial reservoir to support it" (B. Rose, 224). He points to the development of Silicon Valley as a real life example. "You might think that the source of all this change would be the source of ideas about what it means as well. But in true American fashion, Silicon Gulch firms are out to make money, not revolutions" (*Electronic Life*, 7).

This pursuit of wealth above all else leads to the abuse of people. In the novel, Crichton creates the Biosyn corporation to represent the capitalistic sins of biological engineering. They are despised for endangering innocent people with newly developed diseases. Biosyn is also the corporation that persuades Nedry to steal the dinosaur embryos. Crichton's novel illustrates that genetic engineering "is a field driven more often by venture capital than sound wisdom" (Fox, 38). It is a tale "not of mad scientists, but of merely *money*-mad scientists" (Jennings, 15). To maintain a continual intake of money, the wealthy attempt to create new needs in others, convincing them that the only means to happiness is buying luxuries. This in turn, of course, brings the wealthy more money and more power. John Hammond consciously aims to create desperate need in his potential customers so that they will pay $5,000 a day to visit Jurassic Park. Such a motive alienates the classes from each other and further dehumanizes the consumer masses.

Dehumanization is also promoted through the abuse of the workers. Though labor is a positive way for individuals to express themselves, a capitalist society denies people that satisfaction from work. Workers do not get to enjoy the products they make. Instead they get only wages, which they use to buy necessities and luxuries at prices set by those in power. In *Jurassic Park*, paleontologists Grant and Sattler must take time away from the labor they love to follow the whim of John Hammond. Though they do not want to leave their own work, they must visit Jurassic Park at Hammond's bidding because they need him to continue the funding on their expedition. Luckier than most people, Grant and Sattler do work they love and share their findings with humanity. Still, they must depend upon some rich person who knows very little about the work they do and whose only interest is getting even more money and power.

Equally dependent on the whims of John Hammond are the dinosaurs of Jurassic Park. They play a dual role in the Isla Nublar society. First, they are the products of the genetic engineers. But the dinosaurs also represent the lowest, most exploited class of laborers, for it is they who create the entertainment at Jurassic Park. However, they receive no reward or enjoyment from what they "produce." In fact, what they create results from not only their labor, but from the denial of their natural instincts to hunt, to kill, and to migrate. The collapse of this capitalistic society comes from these exploited laborers, who refuse to submit to those in power. Realizing this, those in power begin to contemplate reengineering these workers into more cooperative beasts. Ultimately, they fail.

Only one human character escapes the capitalistic drive to tame him into conformity: Ian Malcolm. This "new mathematician" has broken with traditional ways. He attempts to bring his theory to the real world, and does not hesitate to say what he thinks in all situations. For instance, because he notices and appreciates her, Malcolm continually compliments Sattler on her appearance. He does not worry that such remarks may be considered offensive. He dresses in one color at a time because he finds it liberating. "I don't want to think about *what I will wear* in the morning. Truly, can you imagine anything more boring" (72). He insults science in front of scientists and tells zookeepers that they cannot contain nature. Malcolm fulfills Marx's dream of a human who labors to satisfy his need for expression. He remains intimately connected to what he produces and shares it with all other humans, hoping for the improvement of the species. Unfortunately, the others remain too dedicated to capitalism to hear him and act.

The failure to abandon capitalism leads to the collapse of the society at Jurassic Park. Because the power class ignores the true natures of the workers, it loses control over them. The exploited class seizes power. Ian Malcolm claims that the problem lies in the concept of *inherited* wealth, rather than *earned* wealth. "Most kinds of power require substantial sacrifice by whoever wants the power. There is an apprenticeship, a discipline lasting many years. . . . But scientific power is like inherited wealth: attained without discipline" (306–307). The empowered class is ultimately violent, destroying others and itself.

Dennis Nedry is an example of a member of the empowered class who loses his humanity and his life in pursuit of money. Even as he hurtles toward his death through a torrential downpour, he can focus on little else except his own success. "It was a good plan. . . . This plan was going to make him a million and a half dollars" (194). His behavior has destroyed his ability to interact with other people. He tapes conversations with his business partners so that he can blackmail them. He sacrifices the lives of others to make his escape. He has obtained his power without obtaining the discipline to know how to use it wisely.

Nedry, Hammond, and Wu all die just as they are about to get the money and power they have sought all their lives. Their narrow-minded greed has destroyed their creativity and goodness. Likewise, it has prevented them from recognizing the true nature of others. This failure sets up their demise at the "hands" of the dinosaurs they have created and exploited. Their conceit makes them overconfident and careless, which blinds them to oncoming danger.

The impending danger results from the revolution of the exploited classes. In Crichton's novel, as in Marx's vision, this never really comes to pass, but remains an unrealized dream. At the end, the destruction of the island is complete. The remaining dinosaurs have escaped and freely pursue their nature. But the gothic ending is terrifying because the government engages only in a massive cover-up. No provision is made to stop a similar situation from developing again or to contain the dinosaurs, which still live in the jungles.

Crichton's novel reflects actual social anxiety about the abuse of scientific power by profit-seeking scientists. Anxiety about genetic engineering and the need to control it centers primarily on anxiety about capitalism and how the desire for wealth destroys even the most noble of pursuits. Speaking about the film, one critic hailed the "overdue comeback for a genre once prevalent in filmland: the movie centered on evil at the corporate apex" (Seligman, 174). The comment is equally applicable to the book. Like *Rising Sun, Jurassic Park* has been labeled both a wake-up call and a book that bashes. It is a warning of what will happen if science becomes "almost wholly the handmaiden of big business" (Jennings, 14).

In addition to focusing on the dangers of capitalism's influence on science, Crichton addresses current trends within the business community in his depiction of the dinosaurs and their characteristics. The tyrannosaurus rex, traditional king of the dinosaurs, has been replaced as the ultimate evil by the velociraptor. The large, lumbering corporate power has begun to topple. "Downsizing and diversity are in; constrained hugeness has become a tragic flaw. *Velociraptor* is everything that modern corporate life values in a tough competitor—mean, lean, lithe, and intelligent" (Gould, 54). And such a business is lethal to its competition and to its victims.

Crichton's adventure novel remains unsurpassed for popularity. Novel, movie, and product tie-ins swept the world, bringing dinosaurs and genetic engineering to the forefront of almost everyone's vocabulary. The world's oldest armored dinosaur, "a 10-foot-long ankylosaur 170 million years old" discovered in 1993, was named in tribute to actors who starred in the film *Jurassic Park*: *Jurassosaurus nedegopefenkimorum* ("Jurassic Ankylosaur," 9), which combines the first two letters of the last names of the actors. However, no part of that name is dedicated to the creator of it all, Michael Crichton. Given his often bleak picture of human nature and society, what does the creator of the fiction think about the possibilities that someone could create the same situation in the real world? "I think to make a really radically different, fully articulated, highly intelligent form of life and set it loose on the planet is not a good idea" ("*Jurassic Park, Future Watch*"). In essence, that sums up the novel itself.

NOTE

1. Those who have seen Spielberg's film and who have not read Crichton's book need to be aware that there are significant differences in plot, character development, and thematic context between the two. One must be careful to consider the film and the novel as distinct entities and not confuse characteristics of each. This chapter considers the novel exclusively.

10

Rising Sun
(1992)

Though all Crichton's novels have been designed to shock in one way or another, none has created as much controversy as his 1992 best-seller *Rising Sun*. It caused one critic to claim that "Crichton has turned alarmism into one of the most profitable schticks in the history of publishing" (Denby, 50). In *Rising Sun*, Crichton does not create alarm about humanity's misuse of some high-tech weaponry, as he does in science fiction novels like *The Andromeda Strain* or *Jurassic Park*. Instead, he explores contemporary economic issues in a detective novel. The public's fascination with these issues also helped the 1993 film version of the novel become a hit.

Rising Sun is not the first piece of detective fiction Crichton wrote. In fact, two of his earlier novels won Edgar Awards for best novel of the year from the Mystery Writers of America: *A Case of Need* in 1968 and *The Great Train Robbery* in 1975. Because Crichton did not publish *A Case of Need* under his own name, that novel does not have its own chapter in this volume. Like *Rising Sun*, *A Case of Need* focused on an extremely controversial issue: illegal abortions in the pre–*Roe versus Wade* era. As a young medical student in conservative Boston, Crichton could not risk having his name associated with that subject. When it won the Edgar Award, Crichton panicked. "If anybody found out I had written that book I would be in a lot of trouble" (*Travels*, 80). The book, which was reissued in 1994 under Crichton's own name, shares fictional techniques and social themes with *Rising Sun*.

This chapter discusses five aspects of *Rising Sun*. The plot structure developed from the heritage of the police procedural novel. Its realism and attention to detail lend the novel an authoritative tone. The character development derives in many ways from yellow peril thrillers of the past and from science fiction traditions. The social context in which this novel appeared also influenced Crichton's theme. Finally, the conflicting beliefs about Japanese and American relations provide material of special interest to a deconstructionist.

PLOT DEVELOPMENT

Rising Sun opens as Lieutenant Peter Smith and Captain John Connor of the Los Angeles Police Department investigate the murder of an expensive prostitute in the boardroom of a new Japanese office building. Connor, who has lived in Japan, serves as mentor to Smith as they deal with the Japanese. Their investigation plunges them into a shadow world of unusual sexual practices, cultural conflict, and business wars. Smith learns that the Japanese have influence in every level of American society, from beer breweries to congressional committees, from university research labs to murder investigations in Los Angeles.

The plot of *Rising Sun* derives from its literary heritage. This is the only Crichton novel that is a police procedural. This type of detective fiction centers on the investigations of actual police officers rather than amateur sleuths like Agatha Christie's Miss Marple or private detectives like Arthur Conan Doyle's Sherlock Holmes. The police procedural is a rather recent development within the genre of detective fiction. Its popularity was boosted by the television "cop shows" of the 1960s and 1970s (Symons, 204). Probably the best-known author of police procedurals is Ed McBain. His novels focus on the eighty-seventh precinct of a big-city police force. These novels, more than any other type of detective fiction, are praised for their realism. Though dramatic license must be used to keep the books from becoming as dull as much police work, they still accurately depict cops' attitudes and techniques.

Crichton's mystery plot appeals to readers because of this realism, making *Rising Sun* "infotainment" at its best (Baldwin, 364). The novel seems "as well built a thrill machine as a suspense novel can be" (Nathan, 22). It even includes a bibliography of forty-three sources to which readers can refer if they desire more information. The focus of the police investigation in *Rising Sun* is the murder of blonde, beautiful Cheryl Austin, a young woman from small-town Texas. She wants "the ring on the finger and the kids and the dog in the yard" (69). Achieving this American dream, however, has been sidetracked by the attraction of the $20,000 fees she receives as a high-class prostitute. She lives in an apartment building full of women "kept" by Japanese businessmen for their exclusive use. During a high-profile party at the Nakamoto corporate headquarters in Los Angeles, Austin turns up dead on the boardroom table.

Investigating Austin's murder brings detectives Peter Smith and John Connor into several conflicts. Obviously, they must outwit the murderer so he can be identified and brought to justice. To do this they must try to understand the Japanese culture, including attitudes about business, honor, and revenge. But the Japanese are not willing to reveal their ways to Americans. In an attempt to thwart the investigation, various people bribe, threaten, and misdirect Smith and Connor. Their investigation into Japanese businesses eventually brings false accusations of racism and sexual misconduct. Suddenly Smith and Connor find themselves battling the oversensitive reactions of their government bosses and the press instead of concentrating on the case. The plan to diffuse the investigation seems to be working.

Allying themselves with independent electronics experts, Smith and Connor shift their investigation to the realm of high-tech electronics. Austin's murder was videotaped by security cameras, but the tapes seized by the police had already been switched by the culprits. The Japanese businessmen apologetically turn over what they claim is the original, but Smith and Connor suspect it has been altered. Using computer image enhancement, their team discovers the identity of the true murderer. Although an American congressman is implicated by early scenes in the tape, and actually believes himself to be the killer, later scenes prove that a Japanese man actually murdered the already injured woman.

Their experience within the Japanese business world has taught Connor and Smith that to effectively bring the killer to justice, they must work within that system rather than within their own. They take the tape to a boardroom meeting at the Nakamoto company and play it for the corporate chairpeople. As they face indisputable evidence of their colleague's guilt, they distance themselves from him physically, symbolically indicating his banishment from their world. The criminal, attorney Ishiguro, denies his guilt and leaves the room to smoke on the terrace, but when Smith follows to arrest him, he finds that Ishiguro has already leapt to his death.

Crichton follows his novel's climax with unsettling closing scenes. Although they know they have solved the crime and that the criminal has chosen his own punishment, Smith and Connor receive no official acknowledgment that they completed the case. In fact, they must continue to face internal investigations of their actions. Smith, despondent over the lack of integrity within the department, contemplates resigning from the police force, despite Connor's assurances that things can change for the better. Crichton closes his book with Smith staring down at his sleeping daughter, feeling uneasy in his heart about the world in which she must live.

CHARACTER DEVELOPMENT

Michael Crichton's works have developed primarily from the literary heritage of science fiction. They all follow the traditions of that genre, excelling in plot construction and the creation of suspense. But they also produce characters who often seem underdeveloped. *Rising Sun* is no exception to this pattern. What is exceptional, however, is the critical reaction this stylistic technique earns in this novel. Although reviews of Crichton's other novels often dismissed characterization as weak, it was not a severe problem in the overall effect of his thrillers. However, critics lambasted Crichton's thin character development in *Rising Sun* as racism. The character development in *Rising Sun* is not really much different than in his other novels. Only a few individuals stand out in the large cast of characters. Americans Peter Smith, John Connor, and Tom Graham are distinct personalities. Taken in combination, they illustrate Crichton's concerns with bigotry.

Almost all of the Japanese characters in *Rising Sun* remain underdeveloped. Two Japanese men, Eddie Sakamura and Mr. Ishiguro, the Nakamoto attorney, have distinct identities. But they play roles too small to develop fully. Both seem complex, however. Sakamura appears initially as a fast and loose playboy who enjoys expensive drugs and unorthodox sexual practices. But Sakamura has much more honorable substance to his character. In the end he endures torture and dies in order to save his father's reputation and remain loyal to his employers (115). Ishiguro, though ultimately proven to be a murderer, is a brilliant man who struggles to succeed in two very different and demanding cultures. He simply proves unequal to the strain.

Other than these minor characters, Crichton develops the Japanese only as a group, a "Them" as opposed to the Americans. This echoes an early twentieth-century tradition in thriller fiction, the yellow peril. As Chapter 2 explains, adventure novels presented people from Asia as mysterious, seductive arch-rivals who aimed to destroy American society. Often such stories featured Asians assaulting and even murdering white women. Crichton's Japanese clearly follow this pattern in their treatment of American women. They are full of excesses, as one prostitute explains to Connor and Smith: "It's completely natural to them. I mean, I don't mind . . . handcuffs, you know. Maybe a little spanking if I like the guy. . . . A lot of them, they are so polite, so correct, but when they get turned on they have this . . . this *way*" (70). Critics call this sort of material "the oldest theme in racial fear-mongering, which is that over-sexed men from someplace else are going to take our women" ("James Fallows"). This theme, they argue, has been fantastically outmoded by the movement for equality among races and genders in the last several decades. Crichton's work seems to ignore such social progress.

The characterization of the Japanese as an invading enemy "from someplace else" also ties into a theme prevalent in science fiction, where the enemy is geographically and culturally foreign. It is seen as a group, referred to as "Them." "They" are not appreciated as individuals, but identified by highly generalized characteristics. Crichton's depiction of the Japanese in *Rising Sun* recalls such science fiction enemies. "Crichton's Japanese remain aliens from a distant planet . . . not human beings on a globe shared with other human beings" (Oka, 23). "The Japanese in *Rising Sun* are portrayed as aliens, as perfidious and threatening as the virus from outer space in Crichton's *The Andromeda Strain*" (Greenfield, 637).

In contrast to these characters, the Americans are more developed. Crichton uses them to examine American racism. Peter Smith at first seems the perfect example of a man free of racial prejudice. He struggles to behave well in an often unethical world. He is a single father, left by his political-climber wife to bring up their infant daughter alone. He wants to move his child to a house with a yard. But he cannot because his wealthy ex-wife regularly "forgets" to make child support payments. He has volunteered to work in the diplomatic services of the police department. This job brings him into constant contact with people of different nations and races. The book opens with a poignant picture of him struggling to learn to speak Japanese. As he studies, he is surrounded by his daughter's Mr. Potatohead and photographs that need to be put into an album. This man seems admirably honest and open-minded.

At the opposite end of the spectrum is Tom Graham, the homicide detective in charge of the murder case. Graham is bigoted, verbally violent, and purposefully antagonistic at every possible chance. He insults the Japanese in every breath (9, 42). He degrades lawyers (20). He even speaks about the murdered woman's body in particularly gross terms (30). He is well known as a "racist" (76). Where Peter Smith is open-minded, Graham is closed up tight. He seems to hate everything other than his own opinions and perspectives.

The novel eventually reveals, however, that Smith's apparent acceptance of others and Graham's obnoxious bigotry both result from the same thing: ignorance about other cultures. Their different responses to that ignorance, however, lead to their professional performance. Smith wants to learn about the Japanese. He allows the more experienced Connor to guide the interactions with the Japanese businessmen. He accepts without objection a *sempai-kohai* relationship. This establishes Connor as leader and Smith as student. Graham, on the other hand, rejects any opportunities to learn more about the Japanese, preferring the security of his own opinions. Connor tells Smith that he "has a collection of prejudices and media fantasies. He doesn't know anything about the Japanese—and it never occurs to him to find out" (43). Graham's attitudes ultimately prevent him from correctly solving the crime.

In contrast to Smith and Graham, John Connor has lived with and worked for the Japanese. He knows much about them and has earned their friendship and respect. Though Connor can seem a show-off, reserved, secretive, and "a font of stereotypes" about the Japanese (Gross, 12), he ultimately appears more even-handed than that. He is no Japanophile, or lover of the Japanese. But he is no Japanophobe, or Japanhater, either. He is one of the few Americans who works with the Japanese who maintains this moderate stance. "Working with the Japanese is like balancing on a tightrope. Sooner or later, everybody falls off . . . Connor always keeps his balance" (11). This moderation becomes evident throughout the book as he tells Smith both positive and negative things about the Japanese. For example, he praises Japanese society. "You can go anywhere. You won't be robbed. . . . You're not always looking behind you. . . . It's a wonderful feeling" (119). He also, however, condemns the restrictions of that society: "They are the most racist people on the planet. . . . I got tired of the exclusion, the subtle patronizing, the jokes behind my back" (371). Taken together, Connor's comments do not seem stereotypes. They are complex opinions pieced together through experience.

Crichton reveals very little about these men beyond their roles within the mystery plot. Even the tidbits about Smith's private life do little to develop him as a complex personality. But almost all of Crichton's characters are like that. For instance, Crichton draws a *Jurassic Park* villain as a fat, loud-mouthed slob who binges on candy bars and soda pop. Few critics complained about that. But such thin, stereotypic depictions in *Rising Sun* have led it to be called a "stereotype manual . . . [where] women were whores and neglectful mothers . . . the black security guard a spineless liar, the Hispanics coke-dealing bribers. *Rising Sun*'s moral center, meanwhile, accommodated primarily middle-aged white men" (Kim, 62). Nothing is said, however, about the middle-aged white man who is the worst bigot of them all. No one mentions the Japanese who are clever and honorable. Few critics notice the women of principle and purpose who aid Smith and Connor's investigation.

SOCIAL AND CULTURAL CONTEXT

Rising Sun's connection with police procedurals—a genre known for its realism—combines with Crichton's use of detail to strengthen his bleak depiction of the Japanese-American economic situation. Crichton purposefully uses this genre novel to explain complex economic and cultural issues. Beginning in the 1980s, the United States entered a decline in levels of trade and income. At the same time other nations, notably Germany, Japan, and other Asian countries, experienced enormous success. As a result, an attitude of protectionism, or economic nationalism, grew. This idea "rests on the belief that . . . one country's prosperity comes necessarily at the expense of others" (Lindsey, 40). As America faces Japan's prosperity and its own decline, "the demand for a scapegoat steadily increases. Who better than the Japanese to take the rap?" (Ehrenstein, 12). Thus arose the popular concept of the Japanese as cutthroat, dishonest businessmen. Americans insisted that only unfair economic practices could overthrow American economic power. In order to save their own self-respect, Americans began to deny any responsibility for their own economic decline. Instead, they blamed the Japanese.

However, many held a strong belief that America could not withstand

Japanese success because of its own economic shortcomings. The *New York Times* listed American problems in a 1992 article:

> a capital market that resembles a casino and demands immediate profits; an education system that leaves almost 80 percent of our young people unable to comprehend a news magazine and many others unprepared for work; managers who award themselves princely sums while laying off their workers at the slightest hint of a downturn; a collapsing infrastructure of unsafe bridges and potholed roads; and, more generally, a social norm . . . of overconsumption and underinvestment. (Reich, 24)

In order to overcome such economic adversity, Americans joined together to survive, identifying a common enemy against whom to fight. Japan has become that post–Cold War enemy. American battles with the Japanese have become a very strong "means of defining ourselves, our interests, our obligations to one another" (Reich, 25).

THEMATIC ISSUES

Crichton's theme in *Rising Sun* grew directly from America's cultural response to this threatening economic situation. In his afterword to the novel, Crichton calls upon Americans to face the reality of the current world economic situation and to learn more about our worldwide economic competitors. He chides Americans for whining about Japanese success instead of participating realistically in the economic relationship (394). Clearly he feels that his depiction of both Japanese and American citizens has accurately portrayed a situation of which Americans need to become more aware.

Yet such depictions were not acceptable in the political environment in which the book appeared. Many critics did not view *Rising Sun* as a wake-up call for Americans to mend their own ways but as a racist rage against the Japanese. They voiced an overwhelmingly negative reaction to *Rising Sun*, as a novel and as a film. "Michael Crichton is delivering Japan bashing to the American masses," headlined *U.S. News and World Report* (Tharp, 50). The *Far Eastern Economic Review* called *Rising Sun* a "mean novel" that demonized the Japanese (Awanohara, 36). Another critic claimed the novel read "like war propaganda" (Lindsey, 40). One

Japanese businessman called *Rising Sun* a "Japan-loathing book...
[which] just hates people who are Japanese" (Tharp, 50).

Crichton, however, claims that such accusations further prove American denial of responsibility. In a *New York Times* article Crichton warned that the central issue of

> America's long term economic decline continues to be ignored.... I don't know why we can't talk about our decline, but we can't. We're in severe denial. Instead of talking about that decline, reviewers talked about racism or anti-Semitism or evoked conspiratorial imagery about our economic competitors.... Calling me a racist does not address the economic issues I raised. ("Time for Tough Talk")

Crichton urges his readers to learn all they can about the situation around them, to take responsibility for their future, and to act.

A few critics claimed that, in addition to inaccurately representing the Japanese, *Rising Sun* also bashes America. The most dismaying thing about the book, says one critic, is "the lack of any recognition that American individualism and contentiousness, for all the disorder that they create, might offer advantages and spiritual liberties that orderly Japan cannot.... For all their longing for safe streets and a more productive economy, few Americans want to live the way the Japanese do" (Denby, 51). Crichton's focus on America's failures, its lack of investment and interest in education, upsets many readers.

Not all critical reaction was negative, however. One of the most positive reviews of *Rising Sun* appeared in the influential *New York Times Book Review*. Robert Nathan called it a work of popular fiction which "vaults over its humble origins as entertainment, [and] grasps the American imagination...a bravura performance" (1). He also warns readers to pay attention to Crichton's theme. "Despite the book's provocative tone, Mr. Crichton is no xenophobe, no fool, no ranting bigot. The questions he poses are of great consequence in the debate about America's condition at the end of the American century" (23). Similar questions and themes, also targeting debates about America's future, occur in all of Crichton's novels, particularly *The Terminal Man* and *Jurassic Park*.

A DECONSTRUCTIONIST READING OF *RISING SUN*

In keeping with the explanation of deconstruction that appears in Chapter 6, this chapter examines the multiple meanings contained in

Rising Sun. First, we must identify the opposition upon which the novel focuses. Then we must discover which part of that opposition is valued over the other. Finally we must show how the text fails to uphold that value (Lynn, 263). Such an examination reveals that *Rising Sun* is a complex novel full of contradictions. But these characteristics are what make it so interesting.

At first glance, the opposition central to Crichton's text appears to be the United States versus Japan. While that pairing certainly shapes the plot, it is not the focus of Crichton's work. The opposition of blame versus action is specifically mentioned only once in the novel, but it is nevertheless the central thematic opposition. Crichton states the issue head-on in one of John Connor's first lessons to Peter Smith: "The Japanese have a saying: fix the problem, not the blame" (78).

Throughout the book Crichton says that taking action to solve problems is better than placing blame. Taking action is continually referred to as the central reason that the Japanese have beaten Americans in economic achievement. "In American organizations it's all about . . . whose head will roll. In Japanese organizations it's about . . . how to fix it" (78). When the Japanese act, they follow through and achieve their goals. "We would do well to take the same approach" (394). "*Everything works* in Japan. . . . *Things happen* as planned. The Japanese are educated, prepared, and motivated" (74; emphasis added). In his afterword, Crichton asks his readers to consider adopting a similar approach. The United States needs to "wake up, to see Japan clearly, and *to act* responsibly" (394; emphasis added). Americans, especially the United States government, seem willing to act in Crichton's book. But they cannot stop covering up for themselves. Ultimately nothing is done to change the course of our economic decline.

Eventually, Crichton's "pessimism" proves correct. For though he and his character John Connor continually urge their audiences to act, they spend most of their own time placing blame. By setting his economic tale within the genre of detective fiction Crichton has undercut his own message, for the goal of any detective story is to identify the criminal and place the blame. Action is not taken to improve a situation by preventing the occurrence of crime but to locate blame after the murder has already occurred.

Similarly, the novel seeks to blame someone for disastrous American economics. Although the Japanese receive praise throughout the book, they also take a substantial amount of blame. According to the novel, Americans fall behind in technology because the Japanese keep them there (95). It claims that the United States economy moves in the direction it does because Japanese businessmen control it (214). The American populace never resists this control because they remain in the dark, thanks to Japanese control over the American press (195). The Japanese get away with this by falsely accusing their enemies of racism. Whenever an American accuses the Japanese of anything, they claim the American is racist. Ultimately, Crichton *blames* the Japanese for manipulating the American political climate by cleverly *blaming* us for racism. Blame, not action, is at the center of control.

Rising Sun also blames Americans for their own economic situation. Americans have allowed Japan to take over markets in technology (226). They have lost the safety of their own homes through police incompetence (73) and by tolerating high levels of violence (125). They are poorly educated (199–200) and do not care enough about anything to act (254). Smith asks Connor why Americans don't fully understand the potential economic and social disasters that await them. Connor replies, "Why do they eat hamburgers? It's the way they are" (229). Americans are people who "talk constantly. Who confront each other constantly. Who argue all the time. People who aren't well educated, who don't know much about the world, who get their information from television. People who don't work very hard, who tolerate violence and drug abuse, and who don't seem to object to it" (216). According to Crichton's afterword, Americans are whining, absurd, inappropriate, and unrealistic in dealing with their affairs (393). Even as Crichton warns us to wake up and act responsibly, he continually casts blame on society as a whole. Though *Rising Sun* was called racist for its remarks about Japan, these comments about Americans are equally stereotypical and offensive.

Rising Sun does not deliver racism as much as violent blame. It chides Americans for dedicating themselves to placing blame instead of fixing problems. The only person who escapes blame in *Rising Sun* is Crichton himself, who, no doubt, counts the production of his novel as his way of helping solve our nation's economic troubles. In fact, he acted only to place blame.

Rising Sun is the second of Crichton's novels to be accused of bashing its controversial subject. *Jurassic Park* met with a similar reception in scientific circles. Nevertheless, these books introduce their many readers to new perspectives on certain issues. They entertain and they teach. In some cases, the novel even encourages readers to find out more from nonfiction sources.

11

Disclosure
(1994)

In early 1994, television interviewer Diane Sawyer asked Michael Crichton if he had any questions about what it was like to be a woman. Crichton responded, "Is there something I don't know?" ("Michael Crichton," *ABC News Primetime Live*). Crichton believes that men and women are no different in the way they act or perceive events. "I don't think there's any evidence for behavioral differences in adult men and women. . . . It's never been demonstrated. . . . And I think the experience in the workplace, you know, as women start to have these [powerful] positions, is that they behave very much like men" ("Michael Crichton Interview," *Good Morning America*). Crichton's belief clearly prompted the reversal of roles that lies at the heart of his 1994 novel, *Disclosure*.

Crichton's talent for focusing his fiction on society's most feared and contentious issues—exercised so well in *The Andromeda Strain, Jurassic Park*, and *Rising Sun*—assured this novel plenty of attention in popular media. Book reviews headlined in magazines and newspapers across the country, and Crichton appeared on one television show after another. Movie rights sold even before the book appeared in stores, and the film version of *Disclosure*, featuring Michael Douglas and Demi Moore, opened in December 1994 to much media hype.

This chapter explores the development of conflicts in the novel's plot. It also examines the controversial development of the novel's central characters. The social context in which the novel appeared is also important to note, as it accounts for much of the controversy surrounding the book. The novel's theme rises out of this social context. Finally, a feminist reaction to *Disclosure* is presented.

PLOT DEVELOPMENT

Like most of Crichton's work, *Disclosure* succeeds because of a fast-paced plot, its exploration of hot social issues, and its vivid depiction of futuristic technology. It is essentially a piece of detective fiction, with an amateur sleuth driven to investigation by the need to preserve his own livelihood. In this story, Tom Sanders, a veteran manager at DigiCom, a computer development firm, finds himself passed over for an expected promotion, won instead by Meredith Johnson, Sanders's former lover. When Johnson aggressively tries to reignite the old romance, Sanders refuses, and she mounts a campaign of sabotage to ruin his reputation and career. Though advised against it, Sanders resolves to charge Johnson, his female supervisor, with sexual harassment. The bulk of the novel centers on his attempts to discover and prove Johnson's predatory motives and save his own social and professional life. Critics praise *Disclosure* for its complex plot involving "a hush-hush merger, corporate skullduggery, the cyberspace frontier, and good old-fashioned sleuthing" (Maurer, 16). They also appreciate Crichton's popularized but informed attention to the issue of sexual harassment (Forbes, "Hot Topic," 26).

The plot of *Disclosure* develops several complex conflicts, each involving the novel's central character, Tom Sanders, in some way. Most obvious, perhaps, is the conflict between Sanders and his new boss, Meredith Johnson, who wants to have an affair with him. When Sanders refuses her advances, Johnson becomes enraged and devotes herself to ruining his career. Though sexual in nature, this is basically a power play between two individuals. Johnson views Sanders's refusal as insubordination. If she cannot control him in this, she worries that she will not be able to control him professionally. This creates the foundation of a sexual harassment scenario, where one person tries to use his or her power over another person's professional position to force them into a sexual situation. The interaction lacks the freedom of choice that should be part of such an intimate encounter.

The plot's first twist comes when the sexual harasser, Johnson, accuses her victim of harassing her. This introduces the conflict between Tom

Sanders and social stereotypes of men. Everyone quickly believes John-son's version of the story. Though many of his co-workers have known Sanders for years, they do not believe him when he charges that Johnson in fact harassed him. Most people "have a hard time swallowing the unusual claim that a woman forced herself on a man—and that he didn't like it" (Kadetsky, 78). From his wife's initial reaction to newspaper ed-itorials, Sanders faces humiliating accusations. No one seems able to be-lieve him because they cling so tightly to gender-based stereotypes that men are always sexually predatory. "Why is a 14-year-old girl who has sex with an adult male, why is that statutory rape, but a 14-year-old boy who has sex with a woman, he just got lucky?" asks Crichton ("Michael Crichton," *ABC News Primetime Live*). Crichton's gender-reversal of ha-rasser and victim sets the stage for his theme that the abuse of power is not confined to just one gender. Sexual harassment is routinely defined as "an issue of power and exclusion" (Moskal, 24). Crichton insists throughout his novel that males and females are no different in their tendency to abuse that power. Sanders's main goal in *Disclosure* becomes proving his innocence to a society of disbelievers.

As Sanders attempts to prove his own innocence and seek justice for Johnson's offense, he finds himself in yet another conflict with tradition. This time, he must fight the professional "old boy" network. Here, the management of a corporation will do virtually anything—ethical or not—to protect each other. What is unusual is that the mostly male man-agers pull together to protect their newest member, who happens to be female. The old structures, though designed to protect men in power, guard the newly powerful females just as fiercely. Sanders's attorney explains this to him: "Power protects power. And once a woman gets up in the power structure, she'll be protected by the structure, same as a man" (331). In *Disclosure*, the corporate founder protects Meredith, even though he knows about her past harassment of several men. He calls her behavior errors in judgment. "The point is, Tom, faced with a situation like this, I still strongly support her . . . we have to make allow-ances for women" (320–321). This "illustrates the fact of male institu-tional power with striking clarity" (DeVries). Sanders finds himself at a loss when he is excluded from that power structure for the first time in his life. He must reorganize his value system and search for a different source of power if he is to survive this exclusion.

Sanders now finds himself accused of a crime he did not commit and excluded from the power network he always belonged to. His position is an exaggerated version of one shared by many men in contemporary society. White males, for so many years the exclusive holders of power in society, now find themselves in conflict with new ideals of equal opportunity for women and people of all races. In addition, the women who now have power seem to be targeting men. In *Disclosure*, "not only are men being eased out of jobs they once assumed were theirs by right, they are being abused" ("White Male," 34). Tom Sanders feels "frustrated, resentful, and most of all, afraid. . . . On the job or at home, the rules are changing faster than [he] can keep up" (Galen, 50). For what may be the first time in his life, Sanders will have to fight to save his future.

Luckily, a friend connects him with successful attorney Louise Fernandez, who agrees to represent him in his harassment case against DigiCom. This savvy and determined lawyer guides Sanders through the social conflicts that develop as soon as people find out about the case. On her advice, Sanders sends his family out of town. He learns how to deal appropriately with the sudden shift in his colleagues' behavior. Men whom Sanders considered his friends avoid him and even blame him for the disruption in their workplace. His files, both paper and computer, are destroyed, and his ability to log into the corporate computer system ends.

As in Crichton's other novels, the resolution of the conflict lies in the hero's ability to use cutting edge technology to outsmart his opponent. In *Disclosure*, Sanders accesses newly developed virtual reality machines that depict visually the record and file systems of DigiCom and other companies. Sanders and Fernandez mount the virtual reality machines and "walk" through a simulated storage room, complete with hovering angel who provides help whenever needed. Through this system Sanders locates the files he needs to prove Meredith Johnson's financial and managerial misconduct. In order to cover these up, she had falsely accused Sanders of harassment, hoping to deflect attention from her activities.

In a scene reminiscent of the climax of *Rising Sun*, Sanders takes his evidence of Johnson's guilt to a board meeting of DigiCom and exposes her in front of all the executives. Though she continues to accuse Sanders of impropriety, of attacking her in order to enhance his own reputation, Johnson can no longer fool the corporate leaders, who quietly dismiss her from the room. As the novel reaches its end, things begin to return to normal for Sanders. Johnson will leave the firm. Colleagues apologize for their cowardly behavior. Perhaps the best result is that the vice presidency that had belonged to Johnson goes to the woman who in fact deserved the promotion. The novel closes with Sanders eagerly greeting his returning family at the airport, intent on dismissing the incident and getting on with his personal and professional life.

CHARACTER DEVELOPMENT

As in most of Crichton's other work, character development is weak in crucial respects. The minor characters seem to be essentially stereotypes of the sorts of people found in office environments. Even the main characters seem to exist primarily as generalized representatives of certain types of people. However, Tom Sanders, Meredith Johnson, Louise Fernandez, and Stephanie Kaplan, considered all together, present an interesting portrait of the possibilities of male-female professional relationships.

Tom Sanders is clearly the protagonist, or hero, of the novel. He is the victim of a crime and acts to right that wrong. He is not motivated by revenge, but by a dedication to what is just. He refuses to submit to the threats from his bosses and their lawyer. Instead he risks his career and his family to prove Johnson guilty of her crimes. He resembles the knight in shining armor of adventure tales. He does not simply battle an individual, but an entire society. He champions the idea that everyone should receive the same treatment, for good or ill. However, Sanders is not perfect. He enjoys the power and entitlement he has experienced as a male. He clearly lacks the ability to quickly assess and delicately handle unusual situations. These are the characteristics that land him in his desperate position. "Sanders isn't in trouble because he's naive; it's because he's not good at office politics. He expects moral behavior from people for whom situational ethics is the rule" (Seago, B5). His expectations of other people and his refusal to play corporate games eventually exclude him from power.

Meredith Johnson, on the other hand, is exceptional at fulfilling other people's expectations. She enters office politics with a deadly seriousness. In order to rise from demonstrator to vice president, Johnson has improved her appearance as an executive, but not her competence. She has made decisions that have cost the company millions of dollars but covers them up by blaming other workers. She smoothly produces fake technical language in marketing meetings to cover her ignorance of the actual situation. But knowing her dangerous reputation, none of the knowledgeable engineers will speak out against her. Over the years she has even altered her hair, her face, her dress, and her body language to look like the corporate president's daughter, who was killed in a car accident.

In Meredith Johnson, Crichton has created a remarkable villainess. This vision of a woman as a powerful sexual predator draws intense reaction from almost every reader. Some believe she represents real dangers. "Here we have one great male fear; that women will use their intoxicating wiles to climb the professional ladder and, once perched on a lofty rung, prove even more abusive than male bosses" (Maurer, 16). Others find her merely pathetic. In terms of "corporate gamesmanship, [she is] as much victim, in the end, as villain" (DeHaven, 46). Still others find her too exaggerated to seem real (Seago, B5). In fact, many have pointed to Johnson's character and claimed that *Disclosure* is a book written against women. It has been called "the latest lob in the tide of women-hating which is currently engulfing the United States" (Burchill, 25).

However, two other prominent female characters are contrasted to Johnson throughout *Disclosure*, proving that there is more to Crichton's book than female-bashing. The first is attorney Louise Fernandez. Unlike Johnson, Fernandez succeeds because she is extremely talented and competent at her job. Men like Sanders are surprised by her serious attitude when they meet her.

> He was taken aback by her brisk manner.... She got out a
> yellow legal pad and set it before her. Her movements were
> quick, decisive.... He looked around the office. There was a
> neat stack of bar charts for a courtroom appearance. Fernandez looked up from the pad, her pen poised. It was one of
> those expensive fountain pens. (167–168)

Despite her evident preparedness, Sanders becomes convinced she is the wrong person to help him. He finds that she reminds him of Meredith. Soon, however, he discovers the difference between the faked appearance of competence and the real thing, and his reluctance disappears. He and Fernandez become partners in a moral crusade. Fernandez proves herself to be professional, forthright, and tough enough to survive the attacks of the less scrupulous legal team at DigiCom.

Throughout their pursuit of the hidden motives behind Meredith Johnson's maneuvering, Fernandez and Sanders receive help and encouragement from an electronic mail source known only as AFRIEND. This friend turns out to be the chief financial officer at DigiCom, Stephanie Kaplan. Other workers in the company view Kaplan as a virtual nonentity. "She was a tall, bony, awkward woman who seemed resigned to her lack of social graces" (65). She rarely speaks to colleagues about professional or social matters. "Colorless, humorless, and tireless, her dedication to the company was legendary" (65). Her nickname, Stephanie Stealth, not only refers to her quiet-as-a-mouse personality, but also to her very real power in the corporation. She has a "habit of quietly killing projects she did not consider profitable enough" (52). She is known for uncompromising expectations of others and of herself, and for an unflinching honesty that has hurt her politically in the company. She even beats her boss at golf (65). Kaplan is quick to discover the corporate conspiracy designed to ruin Tom Sanders and to save a multimillion dollar merger. In a variety of ways she attempts to direct his investigation onto the right path. Her efforts enable Sanders to reveal Meredith's illegal and unethical activities. This saves Sanders's job and reopens the vice presidency for a new candidate. Soon Kaplan herself becomes the new vice president for advance planning. Kaplan makes no bones about her motives. They are not emotional, political, or sexual. "Friendships are nice. So is competence" (492). Kaplan clearly promotes equal opportunity, regardless of gender, for those who are qualified to do the job right. She and Fernandez prove that not all competent, powerful women will abuse men.

SOCIAL AND CULTURAL CONTEXT

Perhaps the most interesting aspect of *Disclosure* is the social and cultural context in which it appeared. Through the late 1980s and early 1990s, sexual harassment had become a familiar issue in every workplace and educational institution in the United States. A survey of *Fortune* 500 companies suggested that harassment cost each firm about $6.7 million a year—and that did *not* include litigation or sabotage (Fritz, 4). Despite such familiarity, however, many people still felt confused about the issue. Reports varied on the extent of the harassment problem. For instance, a 1988 study by the Equal Employment Opportunity Commission suggested that 42 percent of women had been harassed at work (Charney and Russell, 12). That same year, a survey by *Working Woman* magazine reported that "90% of women get harassed" (Morgenson, 70). *Forbes* magazine, however, claimed that the number of harassment cases filed in 1988 represented only 0.0091 percent of working women (Morgenson, 70). Some sources declared that harassment was declining (Morgenson, 70), while others reported it was up (Frum, 162). A clear picture of the true extent of the problem was almost impossible to find. Therefore, people who wanted to ignore the problem could more easily dismiss it as feminist hysteria. This caused tremendous social tensions.

Into this hot cultural frying pan, Crichton dropped *Disclosure*, further heating up the mixture by making the sexual harasser a woman and the victim a man. In the afterword to the novel, Crichton insists that this was to allow readers to "examine aspects concealed by traditional responses and conventional rhetoric" (497). The situation described in *Disclosure* does have a foundation in truth, and certainly similar situations have gained attention in the national press. A 1993 article told about a male worker who had engaged in sexual relations with his female boss, then four years later charged her with sexual harassment. The woman had risen within the company with the founder's support. She, in turn, became a mentor to the male employee, guiding him through promotions, while having an affair with him. He claimed that when he refused to continue a sexual relationship with her, she "demolished his office and all his personal belongings, and demoted him" (Kadetsky, 49). The company insisted that this job change was not a demotion, but a transfer justified because *he* had harassed *her*. He hired one of the nation's top feminist lawyers and ultimately won his case. The similarities between this case and the situation in Crichton's book are evident.

THEMATIC ISSUES

In *Disclosure*, Crichton illustrates the idea that the abuse of power is not specifically linked to either gender, despite the common belief that only men abuse others in harassment cases. Men and women, when given power, will use it appropriately or abuse it in about the same proportions. Sanders's attorney Louise Fernandez seems to voice the author's opinions best. "I know there's a fashionable point of view that says women would never harass an employee. . . . but on the basis of facts, I don't see much difference in the behavior of men and women" (183). Women, Fernandez states, "can be as unfair as any man ever was. . . . the figures suggest that women executives harass men in the same proportion as men harass women" (331–332). Nonfiction authors have agreed. "It's not that power is at the heart of the gender issue so much as that gender is at the heart of the power issue. . . . Most of the traits associated with the feminine side of the human coin—passivity, collaboration, cooperation, the use of influence rather than authority—are in fact characteristics that tend to be exhibited by *any* group that is oppressed" (Filipczak, 27). Therefore, traditionally feminine aspects are merely characteristics of people without power. Characteristics seen as traditionally male are really only those connected to power. When women achieve equality in a society, they begin to share the traditional characteristics of the powerful.

Crichton's novel attempts to prove wrong the social stereotypes Sanders must combat to prove his innocence. Talking about *Disclosure*, Crichton claims, "In my lifetime, the way college-educated white women have been perceived has dramatically expanded. In contrast, the perception of males has contracted into an emotionally closed and physically violent stereotype" (Toepfer, 24). Women have promoted these stereotypes, Crichton believes, to assume even more power. "If you can adopt the position that you're inherently skilled in some aspect of relationship—say, intimacy—and the other person is inherently deficient, then you have an unbeatable position of power. . . . This is a control dynamic" ("Men's Hearts," 80).

Women continue this control dynamic by influencing the development of new and unreasonably restrictive social rules of conduct for men. In *Disclosure*, Crichton describes a society in which men are always assumed to be guilty. They cannot smile at, touch, or be alone with children for fear of an accusation. They must even be cautious around their own children in case their wives make unfounded accusations during divorce proceedings (270). Crichton clearly believes that gender-based prejudice has not diminished in society, but has merely found a new target, and he illustrates that in *Disclosure*. In order to really progress, he seems to believe that society must eliminate such prejudice entirely. But the society he depicts in this novel clearly fails to achieve this.

A FEMINIST READING OF *DISCLOSURE*

On examining *Disclosure*, one of the first things a feminist critic would notice would be Crichton's use of ideas from current feminist theory. The novel is, in a way, a critique of contemporary developments in feminism, and expresses Crichton's opinion on those ideas. Understanding those recent theories leads to an analysis of how Crichton criticizes them. The development of feminist criticism, discussed in Chapter 4, took an interesting turn in the late 1980s and early 1990s that directly influenced *Disclosure*. In this novel Crichton clearly suggests that the ideas of traditional feminism do more harm than good to both women and men. Instead, a newer perspective on gender relationships should be developed.

During the 1980s, a split within feminism appeared. It became so well known that even the popular media began to recognize and discuss it. Some feminists retained the original idea that women need special treatment to help them succeed in a society traditionally controlled by men. This is called protection feminism. Some say, however, that this promotes the idea of women as victims who cannot succeed without special help. Others argue that men and women are equal in all ways, and should have equal opportunity. This is called equality feminism. It believes that neither gender should receive special privileges or protections. Women are viewed as "sexual, individual, no better or worse than their male counterparts" (Wolf, xvii). As indicated in the above section on theme, Crichton clearly belongs in the latter group.

Perhaps the most crucial issue that divides these two groups is whether or not traditional protection feminism is appropriate in contemporary culture. In criticizing the dangers of protection feminism, Naomi Wolf acknowledges that women do often suffer as victims. However, she argues, "women must recount the all too real ways in which they are often victimized without creating an *identity* from that victimization" (xvii). This "mirrors the . . . traditional claim that women are children . . . [and withholds] from women the right to be held accountable" (201). Equality feminism argues that women have the power to overcome the obstacles a male-oriented society presents. Women face many of the same conflicts Sanders faces in the novel. They must combat sexual harassment and battle against the old boy network which traditionally excludes them. Equality feminism insists that women can succeed this way.

In *Disclosure*, Crichton represents protection feminism as vicious and riddled with hypocrisy. Protection feminists carry a well-stocked arsenal of stereotypes about men and women that they use, in place of facts and analysis, to fight their political battles. Sanders's wife, Susan, appears to have taken full advantage of the growth of opportunities for women. She is a partner at a large law firm in Seattle. However, the opening scene of Crichton's book shows she feels her professional demands are more important than her husband's. She is also not above using sex to manipulate him into doing something he can ill afford to do. In an argument, she automatically resorts to stereotypes about women's professional situations. She claims she has two jobs, as a lawyer and a mother, even though the opening scene has clearly illustrated that Sanders takes care of the children. She claims she is oppressed as a woman, even though she has employees who wash clothes, cook, clean the house, and babysit (129–130). Her belief in stereotypes about women is so strong that it prevents her from appreciating the advantages she has gained.

Protection feminists use stereotypes to bash men everywhere in *Disclosure*. Even one female member of Sanders's own legal team remains convinced that he did harass Meredith Johnson. She believes he is lying simply because he is a man. Women, she thinks, never act aggressively in sex. When Fernandez asks her if that's a stereotype, she responds, "It's not a stereotype because it's true" (186) and studies have proved it. When Fernandez reminds her that studies have also proved that women are weaker in math and strategic thinking, she insists simply that those studies are wrong. "I see," Fernandez replies. "But the studies about sexual differences are right?" (187). Protection feminists appear to resist negative stereotyping of women on the grounds that stereotyping is prejudice. But they promote stereotypes that fit their political agendas.

Perhaps the best example of this is Constance Walsh, a columnist who writes on "feminist perspectives." She promotes a victim-centered feminism that borders on the ridiculous. Her blind hatred of men often leads her to ignore the truth and even to put down women. So what if Johnson harassed Sanders, she wonders. He only complained because he hates women and hoped to ruin her career. Walsh believes he resents Johnson's power and independence, and has reacted violently to it. "He's a typical man. And let me tell you, before I'm through with him, he'll wish he had never been born" (351–353). According to Walsh, behavior that would be abhorrent for a man is excusable for a woman. This double standard undercuts everything equality feminists have tried to gain.

Crichton's critique in *Disclosure* does not include all feminism. It only objects to the protection feminism that harms women as well as men. *Disclosure* also offers a strong portrait of equality feminism, particularly in the characters of Louise Fernandez and Stephanie Kaplan. Both these women are savvy yet moral in their behavior, and both survive environments riddled with vindictive aggression. They both succeed without receiving any special favors because of their gender. This fundamental aspect of Crichton's novel is almost entirely overlooked by critics.

Crichton ends his novel with a glimpse of the damage protection feminism can do. His final depiction of Meredith Johnson proves both powerful and disturbing. Because Meredith learns nothing from her ordeal, the happy ending remains somehow incomplete. Her prejudiced blindness remains unaffected by any events, even the loss of a job. Meredith leaves DigiCom convinced that she bears no responsibility for what has happened. "I don't deserve this. I've been screwed by the system" (480). She believes she suffers as yet another victim of the traditional patriarchal system run by men. "Women in business have to be perfect all the time, or they just get murdered . . . I was raped by the . . . system" (490–491).

Meredith's insistent denial shows the problem that comes from a feminism that labels women as victims. Such feminism prevents reasonable assessment of situations and appropriate reactions. *Disclosure* indicates that women as well as men can remain ethical and survive in the real world. But to do that they must act to help themselves instead of casting about for someone else to blame. Crichton discusses a similar theme in *The Terminal Man* and *Sphere*. He also develops it in the context of racism in *Rising Sun*.

12

The Lost World
(1995)

In late 1995, Michael Crichton did something which he had never done before in his fiction: he wrote a sequel. *The Lost World* continues the story begun in *Jurassic Park*. More than six years have passed since Alan Grant, Ellie Sattler, Ian Malcolm, and the others visited John Hammond's zoological park on an island off Costa Rica. Coerced into silence by the Costa Rican government, all steadfastly deny any rumors about genetically engineered dinosaurs. They have gone on with their lives.

The Lost World reintroduces Ian Malcolm, the outspoken mathematician and chaos theorist who, it seems, did not really die at the end of *Jurassic Park*. Malcolm is drawn into this new adventure by a young paleontologist named Richard Levine. Levine has learned that the bodies of large, mysterious lizards have washed up on the Costa Rican mainland. He convinces Malcolm and other adventurous volunteers to travel with him to Isla Sorna to observe the animals in the wild. Once there, they must survive attacks by free-roaming carnivorous dinosaurs of all kinds. They must also cope with the profit-hungry scientists from Biosyn, an evil bioengineering firm out to steal the genetic technology for making dinosaurs.

Critics did not react kindly to the novel, although it immediately became a bestseller. Reviewers felt *The Lost World* was too derivative of both Crichton's novel and Spielberg's film. One critic even felt that the novel read, "like a movie novelization: so bereft of plot and characterization in deference to action that it [barely resembles] the entertaining and educational novel that preceded it" (Annichiarico, 91). Crichton acknowledged that writing a sequel presented special challenges because of the enormous success of *Jurassic Park*. A sequel, he remarked, presents "a very difficult structural problem because it has to be the same but different. And if it's really the same, then it's the same, and if it's really different, then it's not a sequel" ("*The Lost World*"). This chapter will examine five aspects of this novel not only as an individual work, but as a sequel to the earlier story. Plot and character development and the novel's debt to generic conventions all adhere closely to the patterns established by *Jurassic Park*. Thematic development differs, however, and the suggested deconstructive reading highlights new directions that readers can explore in this novel.

Plot Development

The plot of *The Lost World*, like that of *Jurassic Park*, develops in the manner of traditional adventure and science fiction. It features an episodic structure, with many short chapters and frequent exciting climaxes. Such fiction relies heavily on conflict and action to keep readers interested. The first conflict begins even before the heroes reach the dinosaur-inhabited Isla Sorna. Even at home, Malcolm, Levine, Levine's co-worker Jack Thorne, and Levine's seventh-grade assistants Arby and Kelly are stalked by a vicious group of thieving scientists from Biosyn. This is the unethical corporation that convinced computer designer Dennis Nedry to steal dinosaur embryos in *Jurassic Park*. Biosyn suspects a lost world of dinosaurs exists, but rather than locate it on its own, it follows Levine and Malcolm. The Biosyn leader, Lewis Dodgson, makes it completely clear to his team and to readers that he will stop at nothing, not even murder, to get the dinosaur technology this time.

Once Levine, Malcolm, and their group reach the island, they enter into conflicts familiar from both the novel and film of *Jurassic Park*. Raptors, T-rexes, and compys roam the island freely and have established a balanced ecosystem there. These scientists hope not to disrupt that environment, but merely to study it, learning as much about the animals as possible during their short stay. But hot on their heels comes the Biosyn team, traveling in a polluting gas-powered jeep and stealing as many dinosaur eggs as they can manage. Inevitably, humanity disrupts the environment, sending protective dinosaurs in search of their eggs, destroying virtually everything in their path.

Crichton designs fast-paced action in order to win the popular audience. "I assume that people are tired, you know, that they have other things to do. . . . I had really better try and grab them and make them turn the page" ("Interview"). This need presents authors like Crichton with a difficult challenge. They must create intense conflict with frequent climaxes, yet keep the adventure story from becoming contrived or unbelievable. In *Jurassic Park*, Crichton established a plotting technique which he continues in *The Lost World*. He continually divides his band of heroic scientists into smaller groups and separates them across the dinosaur-infested island. Then Crichton rotates his chapters among the groups. This allows him to write short, exciting chapters without having the same characters encounter an unrealistic number of dangerous events. This makes the plot more believable to readers.

Crichton also captures his readers' attention by skillfully using plot to build suspense. He does this in several ways. As in other novels, Crichton uses a technique called "the ticking clock" to create tension. Characters and readers alike fear an approaching deadline, which draws ever closer, bringing with it an increased threat. In *The Lost World*, for example, the battered scientists have sought shelter from the dinosaurs in one of the abandoned factory buildings on the island. However, they must leave this safety and travel through the jungle to reach an open plain at a specific time so a helicopter can rescue them. The time left until the helicopter arrives threatens the heroes in two ways. On one hand, it is too long and allows the dinosaurs plenty of time to attack again. On the other hand, the time remaining is too short, and it dwindles rapidly as the heroes try to devise a way to survive their travel through the jungle. In a fierce race against the final minutes, one scientist, Sarah Harding, arrives at the site just as the rescue helicopter takes off. Faced with despair, the scientists now must use their own ingenuity, not reliance on outside help, to save themselves.

Crichton also builds suspense in his plot through dramatic irony. In this situation, some characters and the audience have more information about the heroes' plight than do the heroes themselves. In *The Lost World*, Malcolm, Levine, and the others believe that their only real danger comes from the wild dinosaurs. Therefore, they approach their observations cautiously, taking care not to reveal themselves or to upset the island's ecology. What they do not know is that the industrial espionage team from Biosyn has followed them to the island. Only Lewis Dodgson and his cohorts King and Baselton know the true situation. And, of course, so does the reader.

Suspense reaches its highest points in the novel during situations of dramatic irony. The unsuspecting Sarah Harding arrives in Costa Rica too late to fly to Isla Sorna with Malcolm and the others. On the mainland, she searches for alternate transportation, and encounters Dodgson's group. Readers know Dodgson's evil motives and shudder in dread when Harding accepts their offer of a boat ride to the island. She begins the journey in all innocence, but readers know she may not survive. Later, Dodgson and his crew travel across the island, upsetting everything that the scientists have worked so hard to preserve. They drive a noisy jeep, walk boldly into dinosaur nests, carelessly injure baby animals, and steal unhatched eggs. Readers watch as their careless actions start an aggressive chain reaction that endangers the heroes.

Eventually, all ends well in this fast-paced adventure, at least for the heroes. Crichton treats readers to an appropriately gruesome demise for spy and egg-stealer Dodgson. The T-rex that captures Dodgson does not kill him, but carries him home to the nest where he becomes the training animal for the little T-rexes' hunting lesson. The heroes escape basically intact, leaving the lost world to survive on its own. Affirming the outcome of their adventure, Jack Thorne tells the children, "You see all of us together? That's real. Life is wonderful" (393).

Character Development

As in most adventure fiction, character development in *The Lost World* remains in the shadow of plot development. Even more than *Jurassic Park*, this novel offers groups of stereotypes, including the stuck-up rich man, the Amazonian female, the regular adventurous guy, the computer whiz kids, and despicable villains (Olson, 5). *The Lost World* also draws from the cast of *Jurassic Park*. Malcolm and Dodgson reappear. So also do a paleontologist amazed at real dinosaurs, an athletically able and beautiful female scientist who can treat sick dinosaurs, a practically minded adventurer, children of each sex, and likable assistants who get eaten by the prehistoric carnivores.

Shortly after *The Lost World* appeared, Crichton admitted that character development is not his strong point. "In writing, I have always felt that I don't really understand why people do what they do. . . . So I'm always doing an external kind of description. All I feel comfortable with is what happens" ("*The Lost World*"). Perhaps his feeling explains why plotting always succeeds in Crichton's novels, while characterization often falls short.

The characters in *The Lost World* divide clearly into two conflicting groups. The protagonists, or characters for whom the reader feels sympathy, include the research team headed by Ian Malcolm and Richard Levine. As in *Jurassic Park*, all the protagonists are characterized by their respect for and interest in learning about the natural world. Each of these characters has a different method for pursuing knowledge, but all are motivated by a love for life and a respect for the animal world.

Ian Malcolm is the wisecracking mathematician and chaos theorist who predicted the disaster of *Jurassic Park*. Readers may also remember that Malcolm dies at the end of that novel, but in *The Lost World*, Malcolm assures his colleagues—and readers—that reports of his death were premature. Crichton here employs a technique made famous by Arthur Conan Doyle. Doyle killed his famous detective, Sherlock Holmes, by having him fall over an Alpine waterfall. Years later, when Doyle wanted to write more Holmes stories, he had the detective simply appear and announce that the accounts of his death were untrue. Crichton himself admitted that he mimicked Doyle's technique by resurrecting Malcolm in this way ("The Lost World").

Crichton considered more than Malcolm's popularity when deciding to bring him back for this book. Malcolm functions as "the ironic commentator inside the story who talks about the action as it takes place" ("The Lost World"). Malcolm's first appearance implies that he is divinely inspired. Speaking to a group of scientists in a room that had formerly served as a convent chapel, Malcolm stands at the podium and pauses, "with a shaft of sunlight shining down on him" (3). Malcolm has an almost purely theoretical approach to the subjects that interest him. In this novel, Malcolm's interests lie in the various causes for extinction, especially mass extinction. Malcolm believes that behavior, not comets or illness, starts the chain reaction that leads to the end of a species. However, science has never proved such theories because behavior can only be observed in living animals, not deduced from bones. This interest leads him once again into the realm of the dinosaurs, hoping to observe and solve the mystery. He explains that, "for the first time, we aren't just studying bones. We're seeing live animals and observing their behavior" (170).

Malcolm's focus on theory also seems to limit his ability to cope with real threats in his environment. As in *Jurassic Park*, Malcolm sustains a serious injury during his first encounter with a dinosaur and spends much of this book under the influence of painkillers. The others have to nurse him and carry him from place to place to keep him safe. When the others leave him to rescue the children from the attacking dinosaurs, Malcolm remains in the field trailer shooting up more morphine. However, only in this drug-induced state does Malcolm communicate his theories.

Malcolm is led to the lost world by a young, unconventional paleontologist named Richard Levine. Like Alan Grant in *Jurassic Park*, Levine encounters living dinosaurs and becomes entranced. He respects the creatures for their true natures, even when that involves gory killings or unusual latrine habits. He wants to observe and learn as much as he can. Unlike Grant, however, Levine irritates most of his colleagues (18). Other scientists generally dislike him, though they acknowledge his superior talents in identifying fossilized remains. In addition, Levine commands an impressive family fortune. To him, money is no object, and his research remains unbounded by financial limitations. Generous in the pursuit of knowledge, Levine outfits his expedition with specialized vehicles and pays all expenses for his hand-picked team of experts to travel to Isla Sorna. He is impatient and rash in his decisionmaking, however. Unwilling to wait for his field vehicles to pass numerous safety tests, he travels to the island with only one native guide. Soon he is stranded there, and his panicked call via satellite phone brings Malcolm and the others running, prematurely, to his rescue.

Working with Malcolm and Levine is Jack Thorne, a former engineering professor who has left academics to "actually make things" (58). Thorne's educational career focused on guiding students through precise decisionmaking and constructive action. Once he taped his final exam answers to the high ceiling of a lecture hall and challenged students to retrieve them using only a shoe box, licorice, and toothpicks (58). Thorne now designs expedition vehicles and equipment to meet the specifications of scientists like Levine. When faced with challenges, Thorne lives by the principles he used to teach, making decisions quickly and acting as constructively as possible. When Levine turns up missing, Thorne does not hesitate to mobilize the expedition for a rescue. On the island, he is the first to risk his life to save the others, particularly to protect the children who have stowed away on the mission (149, 291). Unlike Malcolm, Thorne thrives on activity. And unlike Levine, Thorne dedicates himself to others.

Rounding out the scientific team is Sarah Harding, a biologist who specializes in African predators. She and Malcolm had a brief romance after his return from Jurassic Park, but they are now just friends. Harding had grown up poor, but had struggled her way to the scientific limelight by studying lions and hyenas. She is physically beautiful (61) and athletically tough, broadcasting a "rugged but glamorous" (62) image. The image proves true when she arrives in Costa Rica to join Malcolm and Levine's expedition. Unsuspecting, she accepts a boat ride to the island from the Biosyn group. Only a few yards from the island's cliffs, Dodgson pushes Harding overboard and leaves her to die. Despite nausea, freezing cold, and terror (196), Harding swims until exhausted. Though she recognizes the situation as hopeless, still she tries (197)—and she survives. When Harding and Malcolm face death inside a motor home about to slide over a cliff, she carries him to safety despite her own injuries. Perhaps most significantly, she has the sensitivity to recognize a young girl of quick intelligence who, with a little mentoring, can someday achieve great things.

This young girl is Kelly Curtis, one of two children enmeshed in Crichton's adventure. Both Kelly and her friend Arby Benton prove admirable protagonists. They are loyal and dedicated to the adults, especially to Richard Levine who has hired these seventh-grade geniuses to run errands for him. They demonstrate a creative capability with all facets of technology. They also demonstrate resourcefulness in their risktaking when they stow away for twelve hours in storage compartments aboard the field vehicles (120-121). Thirteen-year-old Kelly comes from a rather unstable home life. Her single mother is unreliable at best. She rarely comes home to care for her children, and when she does, she frequently brings a different boyfriend (46, 48). She has been arrested twice for drunk driving (48). Kelly's current problem is a reluctance to go home by herself because the latest boyfriend has moved in, and she finds him "creepy" (87). Kelly wears her sister's K-Mart hand-me-downs, which she washes over and over again in a futile attempt at cleanliness. Kelly's success lies in the sciences and math, where she performs far ahead of her schoolmates. They, in fact, taunt her regularly as a "brainer" (47), but she holds her head high and aims to become like her hero, naturalist Sarah Harding (61–62). With the support of her friend Arby, she endures.

Though a genius like Kelly, Arby Benton is in many ways her opposite. He hails from an upper-class black family that provides stability and predictability almost to a fault. His physician parents dress him like a young professional (46). Arby is only eleven years old, having skipped several grades. Kelly worries that if he skips more, she will lose daily contact with him. Arby is shy around other people, except for his friend Kelly. He constantly tries to fit in with other children but cannot. "He wasn't white, he wasn't big, he wasn't good at sports, and he wasn't dumb" (120). He falls asleep in school because his classes are so boring. However, he revels in the theoretical world of cyberspace. He is an advanced computer hacker and very skilled at figuring out other devices as well. His skill gives him the confidence to lead the adults when their adventure requires technical expertise. Even Thorne, the technological wizard, "was amused by the imperious way Arby behaved whenever he was working with a computer. He seemed to forget how young he was, his usual diffidence and timidity vanished" (72).

The most outstanding difference between these two young adventurers lies in their ability to handle the chaotic aspects of life, about which Malcolm so often speaks. Conditioned by her background to expect the unexpected and to fend for herself, Kelly finds excitement and joy in unpredictable events like encountering live dinosaurs. Arby, whose home environment has prepared him only for stability, enjoys only the mechanized predictability of computer environments. His confidence collapses whenever he faces something unpredictable, like the dinosaurs. He finds it "reassuring to organize, to create order in his life" (153). He loathes the island where "everything was so unknown and unexpected" (154) because he does not know what will happen. The children, like the adults, split into two modes of dealing with reality. Arby, Malcolm, and initially Levine remain more detached, interested in the theoretical implications of life. Kelly, her idol Sarah Harding, and Jack Thorne interact with life in all its glory.

Though they differ in their approaches, the protagonists all respect life and attempt to learn from it. This separates them from the antagonists, or characters who interfere with the protagonists' activities. In *The Lost World*, the primary antagonist is Lewis Dodgson, a "ruthless and aggressive geneticist" (94). His name recalls the famous adventure novel *Alice's Adventures in Wonderland*, written by Lewis Carroll, a pseudonym for Charles Dodgson. *Jurassic Park* introduced Dodgson as a scientist who tested a rabies vaccine on unsuspecting farmers. He justifies his actions without scruple, saying he cannot "be held back by regulations drawn up for lesser souls" (94). He hopes to obtain the secrets of the dinosaurs for a very specific reason—to create living animals. Biological testing on animals has recently become very expensive and politically risky for corporations like Biosyn. Similarly, large animals like lions and tigers have become protected across the planet. Dodgson believes that animals which Biosyn creates would not fall under the same laws that protect other animals. Biosyn would, therefore, have total freedom to use the animals for medical testing or to open a hunting preserve. He brags, *"these ani-mals are totally exploitable.* We can do anything we want with them" (97). This argument alone convinces the head of Biosyn to support Dodgson's latest attempt to steal the technology for creating dinosaurs.

Generic Conventions of *The Lost World*

The Lost World falls squarely within the traditions of the adventure and science fiction novel which preceded it. The detailed discussion of this heritage in Chapter 9 on *Jurassic Park* applies to *The Lost World* as well.

In addition to continuing many of the traditions of the adventure and science fiction genres, Crichton's *The Lost World* draws on a unique ele-ment of literary heritage: a namesake novel. Arthur Conan Doyle, most famous as the author of the Sherlock Holmes stories, also wrote several adventure and historical romance novels. Doyle published his novel en-titled *The Lost World* in 1912. It remains famous today, however, and has recently been referred to as the "granddaddy of the modern-day dino-saur romance" (Olson, 5). In a television interview Crichton acknowl-edged that he liked Doyle's book as a child and felt the title was wonderful (*"The Lost World"*). In 1912, the book introduced readers to a new hero, Professor Challenger, who stood out within the adventure genre. He was an intellectual, a scientist, and an innovator. His insight-ful examination of evidence helped him develop unique views about evolution. Though colleagues called him a fraud and even crazy, he es-tablished a band of academics, hunters, adventurers, and natives to ex-plore the strange lost world. Challenger's character towered above the rather nondescript minor characters of the novel. He was physically tall, but also eccentric in mannerism. Doyle continued his adventures in a 1913 novel, *The Poison Belt*. Doyle's *The Lost World* received another boost in popularity in 1925 when a silent film version of the story ap-peared.

Crichton's *The Lost World* does not draw as heavily on Doyle's work as some of his other novels have drawn on their literary predecessors. For instance, *The Terminal Man* much more closely links to *Frankenstein*, especially in theme. The similarities between the lost world novels ap-pear mostly in details. The fundamental situation of an isolated world inhabited by dinosaurs is, of course, the same. However, in Doyle's book, this is truly a land forgotten by time, not one genetically engineered by humans. High cliffs ring both lost worlds, making access virtually impossible. In both worlds a network of caves cuts through the rocks, allowing adventurers who know the secrets to enter or escape. In both books scientists visit nesting sites and attempt to steal young dinosaurs, causing disaster.

Perhaps the most significant similarity is the scientist who heads the expedition in each novel. Both Professor Challenger and Ian Malcolm are scientists who do not conform to the methodology or beliefs of most of their colleagues. They offer ideas which others often find hard to understand or accept. Challenger and Malcolm abhor the many scientists who "exploit for fame or cash the work which has been done by their indigent and unknown brethren" (Doyle, 39). Both appear early in these books delivering lectures to these other scientists. Challenger thinks of himself as a "high priest" (Doyle, 39) and Malcolm lectures in a former chapel like some spiritual leader (3). These speeches are both interrupted by audience members who question their beliefs. Ultimately, both Challenger and Malcolm wind up on dangerous expeditions with these opposing scientists.

The most significant differences between Crichton's and Doyle's books reflect the times in which each was written. In his *The Lost World*, as in *Jurassic Park*, Crichton emphasizes the importance of respecting the power of all life. Failure to do so brings disaster upon the geneticists in *Jurassic Park* and upon the Biosyn group in *The Lost World*. Doyle's novel reflects a time, however, when exploitation of natural environments was accepted and even encouraged. Big game hunting captured the interest of rich and honorable men. Thus it is not surprising that Doyle's characters fantasize about killing a dinosaur and mounting its head on a wall in their study. Similarly, the British attempted to impose their own culture on the natives. This resulted in a great deal of violence throughout the British Empire. When Doyle's group encounters a culture of ape-men who will not conform to the Englishmen's wishes, the English purposefully annihilate the entire species. Late twentieth century thought condemns both these practices, but in Doyle's time they were accepted. Though Crichton's book reflects different social values, both novels include the accepted practices of their own times.

Thematic Issues

As readers might expect, some of the thematic development of *The Lost World* is similar to that discussed in Chapter 9 on *Jurassic Park*.

Through the character of Lewis Dodgson, Crichton repeats his warning about the dangers of unregulated science. Dodgson does not want to study the dinosaurs. He does not really even want to understand the genetic technology that created them. He wants to engineer them so his company can avoid the regulations that govern animal testing. Like John Hammond in *Jurassic Park*, Dodgson is a man of science who seeks little beyond his own glory and profit. This contrasts starkly to the heroic scientists, young and old, who pursue the dinosaurs out of genuine interest and respect. In Crichton's world, nature seems to recognize those who wish to harm it, and eliminates them. The antagonists meet destruction because of their own misguided actions.

The Lost World does develop other themes which are unique among Crichton's novels. In particular, Crichton uses this novel to explore a particular theory about extinction. Many theories about extinction exist, but most focus on environmental causes. Through Malcolm, Crichton presents readers with the theory that behavior, not environmental influences, leads to extinction. This has impressive implications because it suggests that species, particularly humans, can alter their behavior to prevent their own extinction.

Crichton uses Malcolm to explain the central issues in the prologue to the book. Malcolm states that

> complex animals become extinct not because of a change in their physical adaptation to their environment, but because of their behavior . . . [which] can change very rapidly and not always for the better . . . it can cease to be responsive to the environment. . . . And that leads us to wonder whether the disappearance of the dinosaurs is going to be repeated, sooner or later, by us as well. (xi–xii)

As he does in many of his novels, Crichton seems to be using *The Lost World* to issue a wake-up call about a problem which he feels society has ignored.

Crichton points to "civility" as the most important feature of human survival. As Crichton uses the term, "civility" means an appreciation and utilization of diversity for adaptation. "Unlike other species, we evolve and adapt to our environment through our behavior. . . . There has to be a . . . variable pool of ideas, diversity of . . . ways of thinking, notions of what to do" for people to survive ("*The Lost World*"). Crichton points to the United States, however, as a nation that has lost its civility, its respect for alternate points of view. "We're in a nation that really wants to shout everybody else down" (*"The Lost World"*). Certain kinds of behavior, he notes, perhaps behavior like this, could "produce catastrophic change" (*"The Lost World"*) on this planet.

Crichton's novel suggests that such a loss of diversity will destroy the ability to innovate, which has enabled human survival. Cyberspace technology, like the World Wide Web, will increase interaction among cultures and reduce the pool of diversity which humanity needs to survive. Cultures which have been different for centuries will now become too much alike. As Malcolm explains, "cyberspace means the end of our species" (311). The shrinking global community, hailed by so many as the greatest advancement in human history, actually spells our doom. Sameness across cultures shifts populations into fewer, bigger cultures. Like a large committee in a business, a culture that large cannot innovate. This sameness, promoted by internet communications, mass media, global markets for cars, clothes, and fast food chains "keeps anything from happening. . . . It'll freeze the entire species" (311). Innovation will end along with humanity.

In the end, *The Lost World* offers no clear answers to the question of extinction. In the book, as in real life, the issue remains unresolved. Ian Malcolm, however, seems to believe that human behavior will cause the next major extinction on earth: "Human beings are so destructive. . . . I sometimes think we're a kind of plague, that will scrub the earth clean . . . [and let] evolution proceed on to its next phase" (392–393). This presents sobering thematic material for readers to think about as they finish the novel. But Jack Thorne reminds Kelly and readers that such theories are only fantasies, of little value compared with the realities of life (393). The final line of the novel focuses on what is truly important for each individual: "It's time for us all to go home" (393).

In contrast to this examination of extinction, Crichton illustrates how interested adults like Thorne, Levine, and Harding can give new hope to humanity by serving as mentors to young people. Thorne admires and supports Arby's abilities, even when the child disobeys orders and stows away on the expedition. Perhaps even more interesting is the relationship that Sarah Harding establishes with Kelly. Kelly has hero-worshipped Harding from afar and is thrilled to actually meet the naturalist on the island. The two establish an instant rapport as Kelly tells Harding all about her life (232), about school and home. Through Harding, Kelly hears for the first time that her math ability is wonderful, that her mother is probably wrong, that some men like smart women, and that most of the information people have is incorrect (232–233). This bonding mirrors that of Alan Grant and Tim Murphy in *Jurassic Park*. However, it presents a significant departure for Crichton because he has not represented female bonding before. Crichton's women, good or evil, exist alone in a man's world. Here, however, they work together to contribute toward the future, to survive.

A Deconstructionist Reading of *The Lost World*

Survival—of the individuals on the island, of the dinosaurs long extinct, and of humanity as a species—seems to be the most important issue in *The Lost World*. To read the novel from a deconstructive perspective, we must follow the suggested approach outlined in Chapter 6 and practiced again in Chapter 10. First, we must identify the central opposition within the novel, the pair of opposites which the novel seems to focus on. Then we must ascertain which part of the opposition the author privileges over the other. Finally, a deconstructive reading examines the text for the ways it supports its own opposition. Such a reading illustrates that, despite its apparently positive message about the future of humanity, *The Lost World* also unintentionally suggests that as a species humans have already begun the journey toward extinction.

The important opposition between extinction and survival permeates every aspect of *The Lost World*. The plot centers on locating surviving creatures believed long extinct. Conflicts arise as individuals struggle to survive. Characters theorize, argue, and explore the causes of survival and extinction. Crichton's themes build on this issue and its social implications. This opposition seems the obvious place to begin a deconstructive investigation of the novel.

Crichton's narrative delivers a message about the hope for human survival rather than the potential for extinction. It implies that although adaptation can be difficult, humanity will survive challenges by achieving a balance between stability and chaos. Though most people would choose stability as the more favorable state, Crichton carefully shows that balance leads to success while the comfort of stability makes species stagnant and lazy. *The Lost World* opens with an introduction entitled "Extinction at the K-T Boundary" and a prologue entitled "Life at the Edge of Chaos." These titles point to the theory that successful life balances order and change: "enough innovation to keep a living system vibrant, and enough stability to keep it from collapsing" (4). Too much of either can bring extinction. The book describes evolution as a vast arms race toward balance between aggression and defense. Plants and animals evolve continually to counteract the new attributes of their enemies, to remain balanced (173). As a group, the cast of characters provides an appropriate balance that seems to bode well for the human race. Kelly, Harding, and Thorne reach their peak in response to chaotic and dangerous situations. Arby, Malcolm, and Levine, however, prefer the calm, controllable situations in which they can observe and theorize.

On the central opposition between survival and extinction, *The Lost World* delivers a final, reassuring message. Malcolm offers his oddly comforting theory that if humanity does destroy the earth, it will be because, like a plague, that was our purpose on earth (393). Although an unpleasant portrait, it reassures by removing responsibility from humanity for the havoc it wreaks, implying an evolutionary purpose to our actions. Complementing that perspective, Crichton provides readers with a more pleasant, immediate view: "It's a gift to be alive, to see the sun and breathe the air" (393). There are bad aspects of life, but it is life. Harding's refrain throughout the book, that everything will be fine, rings through. As Harding tells Kelly, "It's always true" (346).

After identifying the author's intended message, a deconstructive reading continues by illustrating how a text actually contains evidence that overturns the position that it intends to promote. Examination of *The Lost World* shows that Crichton's rosy view of the human future is clearly undercut. Humanity has already started down the road toward extinction by failing to provide appropriate education to children.

In *The Lost World*, Ian Malcolm explains that the purpose of evolution is to train the young. Inspired by his morphine haze, Malcolm considers how complex animals like chimpanzees, raptors, and humans adapt. They do not adapt by changing their bodies to suit the environment, as do simpler organisms. Complex animals change their *behavior* in order to survive. DNA has very little to do with the success of a complex species like humanity. Instead, survival depends on teaching and learning, from one generation to the next. Young animals raised without appropriate guidance never become fully functional. This explains why the raptors on Isla Sorna live so viciously, denying their young a chance to feed on recent kills, and often even devouring their young themselves. Without older animals to guide them, only the meanest creatures survive and the species heads toward self-destruction.

Malcolm explains that human evolution has proceeded the same way. Behavior is not instinctive with humans, as with many other animals.

Therefore humanity requires complex societies to develop training for the children (209). Societies make adults—not merely family members—responsible for raising all children. Educating children, Malcolm argues, is "the most important thing that happens" (210). It is one reason the species has survived, "evolved over many generations because it was found to succeed" (332).

The Lost World contains material that suggests that in this area essential to human survival, humanity has begun to falter. Through the children and the adult professors, Crichton explores the failure of our society to properly educate most children, even those most capable of exceptional learning. Smart children brimming with potential, like Kelly and Arby, often find school and their home lives debilitating and boring. They are chastised by teachers for their boredom and taunted by schoolmates for their brilliance. Teachers tell Kelly that although she enjoys math, girls are never as good at it as boys (231). Even Kelly's mother warns her that her intelligence can only harm her in the future because "boys don't like girls who are too smart" (232). Thorne, a retired college professor, recognizes that the kids are still young enough that "the schools hadn't destroyed all their interest in learning" (59). Schools fail because society has begun to put other, softer needs before that of educating children. One outstanding example occurs as Malcolm consults on a museum model of a velociraptor. He suggests it should be made more vicious, more realistic. In response, the museum personnel worry about scaring little kids (73). They ignore the value of the true picture, which "incorporated the interplay of all aspects of life, the good and the bad" (74). As a result, as Harding told Kelly, most of what people think they know is wrong.

This approach to *The Lost World* forces readers to examine the details of the text—details that contradict Crichton's essentially hopeful conclusion. Readers must ask: Is the Lost World the one inhabited by dinosaurs or the one inhabited by us?

Throughout his fiction, Michael Crichton has never avoided tough, controversial social issues. He has admitted that sometimes his work gets a bit compulsive. "The conventional wisdom frequently irritates me. . . . I think a lot of that drives the writing" ("*The Lost World*"). Crichton admits that he wants to be noticed for his ideas, and the influence of those ideas (Jaynes, 63). *The Lost World* fulfills its author's desires, delivering a very unconventional portrait of the "benefits" of global community and the accessibility of cyberspace.

Bibliography

WORKS BY MICHAEL CRICHTON

The Andromeda Strain. New York: Ballantine Books, 1969.
Coma. United Artists, 1978 (screenwriter and director).
"Computers and Human Evolution." *Creative Computing*, November 1984: 189–190.
Congo. New York: Ballantine Books, 1980.
"Conventional Wisdom." *House and Garden*, November 1990: 100–102.
Disclosure. New York: Ballantine Books, 1994.
Eaters of the Dead. New York: Ballantine Books, 1976.
Electronic Life: How to Think About Computers. New York: Knopf, 1983.
Five Patients: The Hospital Explained. New York: Ballantine Books, 1970.
The Great Train Robbery. New York: Dell, 1975.
The Great Train Robbery. United Artists, 1979 (screenwriter and director).
"Greater Expectations." *Newsweek*, 24 September 1990: 58.
"The Happiness Report." *Self*, August 1991: 86–90.
"Heart Transplants and the Press." *New Republic*, 25 May 1968: 28+.
"How to Argue." *Playboy*, December 1991: 128–129, 162, 220–226.
"Installer Hell." *Byte*, September 1993: 294.
"Is Biotechnology Creating a Monster?" *Business and Society Review*, Spring 1992: 43–46.
Jasper Johns. New York: Abrams, 1977.
Jurassic Park. New York: Ballantine Books, 1990.

The Lost World. New York: Knopf, 1995.

Looker. Warner Brothers, 1981 (screenwriter and director).

"Men's Hearts: They Say We Don't Have Feelings." *Playboy*, February 1989: 68–70.

"Mousetrap." *Life*, January 1984: 116–126.

"Panic in the Sheets." *Playboy*, January 1988: 142–143, 181–184.

Physical Evidence. Columbia, 1989 (director).

Pursuit. ABC-TV, 1972 (director).

Rising Sun. New York: Ballantine Books, 1992.

Runaway. Tri-Star Pictures, 1984 (director).

Sphere. New York: Ballantine Books, 1987.

The Terminal Man. New York: Ballantine Books, 1972.

"Time for Tough Talk in the Land of the Setting Sun." *New York Times*, 10 August 1992: A17.

Travels. New York: Ballantine Books, 1988.

"Travels with My Karma." *Esquire*, May 1988: 94–105.

Westworld. Metro-Goldwyn-Mayer, 1973 (director and writer).

Writing as Michael Douglas (with brother Douglas Crichton)

Dealing: Or, The Berkeley-to-Boston Forty-Brick Lost-Bag Blues. New York: Knopf, 1971.

Writing as Jeffrey Hudson

A Case of Need. New York: New American Library, 1968. Reissued under Michael Crichton. New York: Dutton, 1994.

Writing as John Lange

Binary. New York: Knopf, 1971.

Drug of Choice. New York: New American Library, 1970.

Easy Go. New York: New American Library, 1968.

Grave Descend. New York: New American Library, 1970.

Odds On. New York: New American Library, 1966.

Scratch One. New York: New American Library, 1967.

The Venom Business. New York: New American Library, 1969.

Zero Cool. New York: New American Library, 1969.

WORKS ABOUT MICHAEL CRICHTON

General Information

Alloway, Lawrence. "Art." *Nation*, 26 November 1977: 571–572.

Bart, Peter. "King of 'High Concept.'" *Variety*, 1 March 1993: 3–7.

Bosworth, Patricia. "Touring the Altered States." *New York Times Book Review*, 26 June 1988: 30.

Callendar, Newgate. *"Binary."* *New York Times Book Review*, 20 August 1972: 26–27.

Cockburn, Alexander. "Gossip and Death." *Interview*, May 1988: 120–121.

"Crichton's Writing Again to Hit the Screen." *Showbiz Today*. Cable News Network. 25 June 1993.

Dargis, Manhola. "Law of Desire." *Village Voice*, 7 February 1989: 68.

Darrach, Brendan. "Andromeda's Author Casts Long Shadow." *Life*, 3 March 1972: 65.

Goodwin, Donald W. *"A Case of Need."* *American Journal of Psychiatry* 150, no. 12 (December 1993): 1886.

Hone, Joseph. "Into the Nether World." *Times Literary Supplement*, 21–27 October 1988: 1168.

"A How-to for Have-nots." *Time*, 24 October 1983: 57.

Hubin, Allen J. *"A Case of Need."* *New York Times Book Review*, 18 August 1968: 20.

Kahn, Joseph P. "Talking to Crichton." *Vogue*, August 1988: 288.

Kauffman, Stanley. "Midsummer Roundup." *New Republic*, 16 August 1993: 24.

Kroll, Jack. "Review of *Runaway*." *Newsweek*, 17 December 1984: 84.

Meyers, Kate. "Playing Doctor." *Entertainment Weekly*, 9 December 1994: 18–30.

"Michael Crichton." *ABC News Primetime Live*. ABC. 6 January 1994.

"Michael Crichton and John Wells Interview." *The Today Show*. NBC. 18 November 1994.

"Michael Crichton Interview." *Good Morning America*. ABC. 13 January 1994.

Robinson, Jack. "People Are Talking About . . . " *Vogue*, 15 September 1970: 100–101.

Rose, Barbara. "Hollywood Gets a New Man." *Vogue*, September 1973: 186, 220–224.

Rotondaro, Fred. "A Case of Need." *Best Sellers*, 15 August 1968: 207–208.

Sauter, Eric. "A Tall Storyteller." *Saturday Review*, November/December 1984: 20–25.

Schwed, Mark, and Deborah Starr Seibel. *"ER: The Smash Hit America Talks About the Next Day."* *TV Guide*, 19 November 1994: 13–20.

Staples, E. B. "Michael Crichton." *Creative Computing*, February 1985: 26–28.

Biographical Information

Chambers, Andrea. "Author-Director Michael Crichton Is a Master of Multimedia Monkey Business." *People Weekly*, 16 February 1981: 94–98.
Fiori, Pamela. "Endless Journey." *Travel and Leisure*, October 1988: 59.
Heller, Zoe. "The Admirable Crichton." *Vanity Fair*, January 1994: 32–49.
James, Geoffrey. "Five Personal Odysseys." *Maclean's*, 15 August 1988: 50–51.
"Michael Crichton." *Contemporary Authors*. New Revision Series. 40: 99–102.
"Michael Crichton." *Contemporary Literary Criticism* 54: 62–77.
"Michael Crichton." *Current Biography* (yearbook). 1976: 100–103.
"Michael Crichton." *Current Biography*. November 1993: 10–14.

REVIEWS AND CRITICISM

The Andromeda Strain

Cook, Alexander. "The Andromeda Strain." *Commonweal*, 9 August 1969: 493–494.
Donlan, Dan. "Experiencing the *Andromeda Strain*." *English Journal*, September 1974: 72–73.
Sheppard, R.Z. "Crichton Strain." *Time*, 8 May 1972: 87–88.
Shickel, Richard. *"The Andromeda Strain."* *Harper's*, August 1969: 97.

The Terminal Man

Coyne, John R., Jr. "Suspense and Insomnia." *National Review*, 23 June 1972: 700–701.
Edwards, Thomas R. "People in Trouble." *New York Times Book Review*, 20 July 1972: 20–22.
Weeks, Edward. "The Terminal Man." *Atlantic Monthly*, May 1972: 108–110.

The Great Train Robbery

Geduld, Harry M. "Review of *The Great Train Robbery*." *Humanist*, May-June 1979: 65.
Weeks, Edward. *"The Great Train Robbery."* *Atlantic Monthly*, July 1975: 80.

Eaters of the Dead

Sullivan, Jack. "Eaters of the Dead." *New York Times Book Review*, 26 April 1976: 22.

Sphere

Collins, Michael. "Summer Thrillers from Three Masters." *Book World (Washington Post)*, 14 June 1987: 1, 14.

Forbes, Malcolm S., Jr. "More than Labor Day Lite: *Congo/Sphere* by Michael Crichton." *Forbes*, 13 September 1993: 26.

McKinley, Robin. "Anybody Home?" *New York Times Book Review*, 12 July 1987: 18.

Congo

Blewitt, Justin. "Congo." *Best Sellers*, February 1981: 388.

Chambers, Andrea. "Author-Director Michael Crichton Is a Master of Multimedia Monkey Business." *People Weekly*, 16 February 1981: 94–98.

Forbes, Malcolm S., Jr. "More than Labor Day Lite: *Congo/Sphere* by Michael Crichton." *Forbes*, 13 September 1993: 26.

Hayes, Harold. "If Apes Could Talk." *New York Times Book Review*, 7 December 1980: 13, 53.

Jurassic Park

Begley, Sharon. "Here Come the DNAsaurs." *Newsweek*, 14 June 1993: 56–61.

Byrne, Gregory. "As *Jurassic Park* Premieres, Educators Hope Dino-mania Will Invigorate Science Teaching." *Education Week*, 2 June 1993: 6–7.

"Could *Jurassic Park* Become a Reality?" *Science and Technology Week*. Cable News Network. 12 June 1993.

"Could We and Should We Recreate the Dinosaur?" *Nightline*. ABC News. 10 June 1993.

Echikson, William. "Sacrebleu! American Dinosaurs." *Fortune*, 29 November 1993: 16.

Forbes, Malcolm S., Jr. "Dinosaur Thinking." *Forbes*, 21 June 1993: 24.

Fox, Tom. "As a Book or Film, *Jurassic Park* Ought to Provoke Lively Debate." *National Catholic Reporter*, 28 May 1993: 38.

Gross, Ken. "Michael Crichton Sends in the Clones, Giving Dinosaurs a Chance to Party Hearty in a Scary New Sci-Fi Fantasy." *People Weekly*, 19 November 1990: 129–130.

Jennings, Gary. "Pterrified by Pterodactyls." *New York Times Book Review*, 11 November 1990: 14–15.

"Jurassic Ankylosaur Named for Actors." *Lapidary Journal*, April 1993: 9.

"*Jurassic Park*." *Future Watch*. Cable News Network. 12 June 1993.

"*Jurassic Park*: Morality Play?" CNN and Company. CNN. 13 June 1993.

"Mayhem in *Jurassic Park*." *Good Morning America*. ABC. 14 June 1993.

Palmer, Douglas. "Dr. Faustus Meets the Dinosaurs." *New Scientist*, 3 July 1993: 43–44.

Place, Vanessa. "Supernatural Thing." *Film Comment*, September 1993: 8–10.

"Send in the Clones." *Nation*, 12 July 1993: 49.

Skolnick, Andrew A. "*Jurassic Park*." *Journal of the American Medical Association* 270, no. 10 (September 1993): 1252–1254.

Skow, John. "Dino DNA." *Time*, 12 November 1992: CT9.

Uhlir, Paul F. "A Parable on Science and Technology." *Issues in Science and Technology*, Fall 1993: 92–96.

Welsch, Roger L. "Rex Rated." *Natural History*, December 1993: 28–29.

Rising Sun

Anse, David. "Cross-Cultural Crime Story." *Newsweek*, 2 August 1993: 55.

"Asian-Americans Angry at Stereotypes in *Rising Sun*." *Showbiz Today*. CNN. 8 April 1993.

Awanohara, Susumu. "Ethno-Thriller: *Rising Sun* by Michael Crichton." *Far Eastern Economic Review*, 19 March 1992: 36–37.

Baldwin, Frank. "The Japanese: Number One Villains?" *Christianity and Crisis*, 19 October 1992: 364–366.

"Bashing *Rising Sun*." *Rolling Stone*, 2 September 1993: 69.

Brown, Georgia. "In the Realm of the Sempai." *Village Voice*, 3 August 1993: 53.

Buruma, Ian. "It Can Happen Here: *Rising Sun* by Michael Crichton." *New York Times Book Review*, 23 April 1992: 3–4.

Canby, Vincent. "*Rising Sun*: A Tale of Zen and Xenophobia in Los Angeles." *New York Times*, 30 July 1993: C1.

Denby, David. "Dim Sun." *New York*, 2 August 1993: 50–51.

Ehrenstein, David. "War Business." *Sight and Sound*, October 1993: 12–13.

Eisenstadt, Gale. "*Rising Sun*." *Forbes*, 9 November 1992: 284–286.

Greenfield, Karl Taro. "Return of the Yellow Peril." *Nation*, 11 May 1992: 636–638.

Gross, Neil. "A Cop and a Villain Called Japan." *Business Week*, 10 February 1992: 12.

Hosenball, Mark. "Murder on the Protectionist Front." *Wall Street Journal*, 13 March 1992: A9.

"Is New Movie *Rising Sun* Racist?" *All Things Considered*. National Public Radio. 7 August 1993.

"James Fallows Re-reviews *Rising Sun*." *Morning Edition*. National Public Radio. 30 August 1993.

"Japanophobia: Theydunnit." *Economist*, 22 February 1992: 86.

Kim, David D. "Dark Shadows: *Rising Sun*." *Village Voice*, 10 August 1993: 62.

Landro, Laura. "Controversy Brews over Novel Sharply Critical of Japan." *Wall Street Journal*, 16 August 1991: B1.

Lazare, Daniel. "Japan Bashing: *Rising Sun* by Michael Crichton." *Tikkun*, November 1992: 68–69.

Lehmann-Haupt, Christopher. "Investigating a Murder Japan Wants Unsolved." *New York Times*, 30 January 1992: C19.

Lindsey, Brink. "Samurai and Sexual Deviants: *Rising Sun* by Michael Crichton." *Reason*, December 1992: 40–42.

McCarthy, Todd. "*Sun* Gets Watered Down." *Variety*, August 1993: 43.

Nathan, Robert. "*Rising Sun* by Michael Crichton." *New York Times Book Review*, 9 February 1992, sec. 7: 1+.

Novak, Ralph. "*Rising Sun*." *People Weekly*, 2 August 1993: 17.

———. "*Rising Sun* by Michael Crichton." *People Weekly*, 16 March 1992: 23.

Oka, Takashi. "Wake-up Call for Uncle Sam-san." *World Monitor*, March 1992: 22–23.

Pang, Roger M. "Editorial Notebook: *Rising Sun* Is Old Business." *New York Times*, 9 August 1993: A14.

Rapoport, Carla. "The Rights and Wrongs of *Rising Sun*." *Fortune*, 23 March 1992: 125–126.

Reich, Robert B. "Is Japan Really Out to Get Us?" *New York Times Book Review*, 9 February 1992: 1, 24–25.

Schwartz, John. "Whodunnit? The Japanese." *Newsweek*, 17 February 1992: 64.

Seligman, Daniel. "Return of the Evil Businessman." *Fortune*, 31 May 1993: 174–175.

Shapiro, Michael. "Is *Rising Sun* a Detective Story or Jeremiad?" *New York Times*, 25 July 1993, sec. 2: 9.

Shickel, Richard. "Cultural Confusions." *Time*, 7 August 1993: 56–57.

Skow, John. "Setting Sam." *Time*, 24 February 1992: 63.

Disclosure

Ascher-Walsh, Rebecca, and Benjamin Svetkey. "He Said, She Said." *Entertainment Weekly*, 16 December 1994: 22–32.

Barr, Christopher. "Virtually Inspired." *PC Magazine*, 12 April 1994: 29.

Burchill, Julie. "Sometime After Dinosaurs, God Created Woman." *Spectator*, 22 January 1994: 25–27.

Chase, Chris. "Books: *Disclosure* by Michael Crichton." *Cosmopolitan*, January 1994: 18.

Collins, Gail. "What Disclosure Doesn't Reveal." *Working Woman*, May 1994: 100.

Connelly, Julie. "A Crock of Crichton." *Fortune*, 21 February 1994: 108.

DeHaven, Tom. "Lady Boss." *Entertainment Weekly*, 21 January 1994: 46–47.

DeVries, Mark. "Power Staying in the Hands of Men." *The Grand Rapids Press*, 13 February 1994: K7.

Dorning, Mike. "Tyrannosaurus Sex." *Chicago Tribune*, 27 January 1994: B1, 3.

Dowd, Maureen. "Women Who Harrass Too Much." *New York Times Book Review*, 23 January 1994: 7.

Forbes, Malcolm S., Jr. "Hot Topic, Hot Book." *Forbes*, 14 February 1994: 26.

Getling, Josh. "Sex Harassment with a Twist." *Detroit Free Press*, 23 January 1994: A5.

Goldner, Diane. "Michael Crichton: The Plot Thickens." *USA Weekend*, 7–9 January 1994: 4–6.

Jaynes, Gregory. "Pop Fiction's Prime Provocateur." *Time*, 10 January 1994: 52–54.

Lawlor, Julia. "Dark Side of Women Seen as More Move into Top Positions." *Detroit Free Press*, 23 January 1994: A5.

Maurer, Harry. "A Screed in Thriller's Clothing." *Business Week*, 31 January 1994: 16.

Max, D. T. "H'wood Gropes for *Exposure*." *Variety*, 25 January 1993: 1, 153.

Pasternak, Ceel. "Talking About Best Sellers." *HR Magazine*, June 1994: 22–24.

Seago, Kate. "Michael Crichton's Latest Book Probes Use of Corporate Power." *Kalamazoo Gazette*, 2 February 1994: B5.

Squire, Susan. "Office Intercourse." *Bazaar*, October 1994: 136–138.

Toepfer, Susan. "*Disclosure*." *People Weekly*, 17 January 1994: 24–25.

The Lost World

Annichiarico, Mark. "Review of *The Lost World*." *Library Journal*, 15 September 1995: 91.

Doyle, Arthur Conan. *The Lost World*. San Francisco: Chronicle Books, 1989. Originally published in 1912.

"Interview with Michael Crichton." *Larry King Live*. CNN. 22 September 1995.

Jaynes, Gregory. "Meet Mister Wizard." *Time*, 25 September 1995: 60–67.

Jones, Malcolm, Jr. "Publishers' Sweepstakes." *Newsweek*, 18 September 1995: 78–80.

"*The Lost World*." *Charlie Rose*. PBS. 22 September 1995.

Olson, Ray. "Review of *The Lost World*." *Booklist*, 1 September 1995: 5.

Steinberg, Sybil S. "Review of *The Lost World*." *Publishers Weekly*, 21 August 1995: 48.

Toepfer, Susan. "Review of *The Lost World*." *People Weekly*, 18 September 1995: 37.

OTHER SECONDARY SOURCES

Adams, Hazard. *Critical Theory Since Plato*. Rev. ed. Fort Worth: Harcourt Brace Jovanovich College Publishers, 1992.

"The Attractiveness Factor." *Psychology Today*, May/June 1994: 16–17.

Barnes, Annette. "Female Criticism: A Prologue." In *The Authority of Experience: Essays in Feminist Criticism*. Ed. Arlyn Diamond and Lee R. Edwards. Amherst: Massachusetts University Press, 1977. 1–15.

Becker, Alida. "To Make America Wake Up." *New York Times*, 9 February 1992: A7, 23.

Berger, Harold L. *Science Fiction and the New Dark Age*. Bowling Green, Ohio: Bowling Green University Popular Press, 1976.

Bhagwati, Jagdish. *Protectionism*. Cambridge, Mass.: MIT Press, 1988.

Brewster, Todd. "The Rising Sun Meets the Big Sky." *Time*, 29 April 1991: 17–18.

Burress, Charles. "Don't Pity Japan's Part-Time Rice Farmers." *New York Times*, 3 September 1992: A22.

Cawelti, John G. *Adventure, Mystery, and Romance*. Chicago: University of Chicago Press, 1976.

Charney, Dara A., and Ruth C. Russell. "An Overview of Sexual Harassment." *American Journal of Psychiatry*, January 1994: 10–17.

Clareson, Thomas D. "The Emergence of Science Fiction: The Beginnings to the 1920s." In *Anatomy of Wonder*. Ed. Neil Barron. New York: Bowker, 1981. 3–87.

DeBolt, Joe, and John R. Pfeiffer. "The Modern Period: 1938–1980." In *Anatomy of Wonder*. Ed. Neil Barron. New York: Bowker, 1981. 125–334.

"Dino-mite Driven." *Advertising Age*, 20 December 1993: 12.

"Dinosaur Popularity Symbol of Cultural Needs." *Weekend Edition*. National Public Radio. 11 July 1993.

Dixon, Bernard. "Scientists and Their Image." *British Medical Journal* (International), 24 July 1993: 268.

Eutychus. "The Jurassic Church Comes of Age." *Christianity Today*, 4 October 1993: 6.

Faludi, Susan. *Backlash: The Undeclared War Against American Women*. New York: Crown, 1991.

Filipczak, Bob. "Is It Getting Chilly in Here?" *Training*, February 1994: 25–30.

"Film Reviews." *Variety*, 25 January 1989: 14.

Fitzgerald, Kate. "*Jurassic Park* Blitz: It's (Pre) Historic!" *Advertising Age*, 17 May 1993: 1, 46.

Frank, Frederick S. "The Early Gothic: 1762–1824." In *Horror Literature: A Reader's Guide*. Ed. Neil Barron. New York: Garland, 1990. 3–57.

Freifeld, Karen. "Sexual Harassment at Work." *New Woman*, November 1989: 116–119.

Fritz, Norma R. "Sexual Harassment and the *Working Woman.*" *Personnel*, February 1989: 4–8.

Fromm, Erich. *The Crisis of Psychoanalysis.* New York: Holt, 1970.

Frum, David. "Speed Brake." *Forbes*, 11 October 1993: 162.

Galen, Michele. "White, Male, and Worried." *Business Week*, 31 January 1994: 50–55.

Giles, Jeff. "Coming to a Toy Store Near You." *Newsweek*, 14 January 1993: 64–65.

Gould, Stephen Jay. "Dinomania." *New York Review of Books*, 12 August 1993: 51–56.

Grumbach, Doris. "Fine Print." *New Republic*, 7 June 1975: 30–31.

Guerin, Wilfren L., et al. *A Handbook of Critical Approaches to Literature.* 3rd ed. Oxford: Oxford University Press, 1992.

Hamilton, Joan O.C. "Who's Afraid of *Jurassic Park*? Biotech Ought to Be." *Business Week*, 7 June 1993: 34.

Harper, Ralph. *The World of the Thriller.* Baltimore: Johns Hopkins University Press, 1974.

Hoppenstand, Gary. "Yellow Devil Doctors and Opium Dens: The Yellow Peril Stereotype in Mass Media Entertainment." In *Popular Culture: An Introductory Text.* Ed. Jack Nachbar and Kevin Lause. Bowling Green, Ohio: Bowling Green University Popular Press, 1992. 277–291.

Huntington, John. "The Science Fiction of H. G. Wells." In *Science Fiction: A Critical Guide.* Ed. Patrick Parrinder. New York: Longman, 1979. 34–51.

Kadetsky, Elizabeth. "He Admits He Slept with His Boss . . . " *Working Woman*, October 1993: 47–49, 78–79.

Kindel, Stephen. "(No Longer) Rising Sun?" *Financial World*, 14 September 1993: 22–23.

King, Thomas R. "Monster Mash: *Jurassic Park* Offers a High-Stakes Test of Hollywood Synergy." *Wall Street Journal*, 10 February 1993: A1.

Kirchner, Jill. "What Can Women Watch This Summer?" *Glamour*, July 1993: 116.

Lohr, Steve. "The Nation: Who Will Control the Digital Flow?" *New York Times*, 17 October 1993, sec. 4: 1.

Lynn, Steven. "A Passage into Critical Theory." *College English* 52 (1990): 258–271.

Maddocks, Melvin. "New Note: The Novel as Sci-Non-Fi." *Life*, 30 May 1969: 15.

Maher, Thomas E., and Yim Yu Wong. "The Impact of Cultural Differences on the Growing Tensions Between Japan and the United States." *Advanced Management Journal*, Winter 1994: 40–46.

Maloff, Saul. "A Nasty Little Prig." *New Republic*, 6 February 1971: 25–26.

Marcus, Steven J. "Climbing Down from the Pedestal." *Technology Review*, August 1993: 5.

Marx, Karl. "A Contribution to the Critique of Political Economy." In Adams. 625–627.

Morgenson, Gretchen. "Watch That Leer; Stifle That Joke." *Forbes,* 15 May 1989: 69–72.

Moskal, Brian S. "Sexual Harassment '80s-Style." *Industry Week,* 3 July 1989: 22–27.

Moskowitz, Sam. *Explorers of the Infinite.* Westport, Conn.: Hyperion Press, 1963.

Murfin, Ross C. "What Is Deconstruction?" In *A Portrait of the Artist as a Young Man: A Case Study in Contemporary Criticism.* New York: St. Martin's Press, 1993. 326–335.

———. "What Is Feminist Criticism?" In *A Portrait of the Artist as a Young Man: A Case Study in Contemporary Criticism.* New York: St. Martin's Press, 1993. 295–302.

———. "What Is Psychoanalytic Criticism?" In *A Portrait of the Artist as a Young Man: A Case Study in Contemporary Criticism.* New York: St. Martin's Press, 1993. 235–246.

Murray, Kathleen. "At Work: A Backlash on Harassment Cases." *New York Times,* 18 September 1994, sec. 3: 23.

Mutter, John. " 'Grishamizing' Crichton—And Now on to Rice." *Publishers Weekly,* 6 December 1993: 24–26.

Neilson, Keith. "Contemporary Horror Fiction: 1950–1988." In *Horror Literature: A Reader's Guide.* Ed. Neil Barron. New York: Garland, 1990. 160–326.

Passell, Peter. "The Risks for Clinton in His New Trade Policy Toward Japan." *New York Times,* 17 June 1993: D2.

Pener, Degen. "Egos and Ids: Author vs. Author." *New York Times,* 25 July 1993, sec. 9: 4.

Pym, John. "Review of *Coma.*" *Sight and Sound,* Summer 1978: 193–194.

Rafferty, Diane. "The Dress as Film Star." *New York Times,* 25 July 1993, sec. 9: 10.

"The Real Jurassic Park." *Nova.* Prod. David Dugan. PBS. WGBH, Boston. 9 November 1993.

Rich, Frank. "Horror Stories." *New York Times Magazine,* 4 July 1993: 6.

Rose, Lois, and Stephen Rose. *The Shattered Ring.* Richmond, Va: John Knox Press, 1970.

Rosen, Sheri. "Get Wired Now." *IABC Communication World,* November 1993: 40.

Ross, Andrew. "New Age Technoculture." In *Cultural Studies.* Ed. Laurence Grossberg et al. New York: Routledge, 1992. 531–548.

Sanders, Scott. "The Disappearance of Character." In *Science Fiction: A Critical Guide.* Ed. Patrick Parrinder. New York: Longman, 1979. 131–147.

Saxton, Josephine. "Science Fiction: Pie in the Sky." *New Statesman,* 15 January 1988: 41.

Schwartz, Sheila. "Science Fiction: Literature for Our Times." In *The Popular Culture Reader.* Ed. Jack Nachbar and John L. Wright. Bowling Green, Ohio: Bowling Green University Popular Press, 1977. 341–350.

Selbert, Pamela. "Dig Those Dinos." *Lapidary Journal,* July 1993: 77–84.

Selden, Raman. *Practicing Theory and Reading Literature: An Introduction.* Lexington: University Press of Kentucky, 1989.

Selden, Raman, and Peter Widdowson. *A Reader's Guide to Contemporary Literary Theory.* 3rd ed. Lexington: University Press of Kentucky, 1993.

Sheehan, Henry. "The Fears of Children." *Sight and Sound,* July 1993: 10.

Showalter, Elaine. "Toward a Feminist Poetics." In Adams. 1223–1233.

Spinrad, Norman. *Science Fiction in the Real World.* Carbondale: Southern Illinois University Press, 1990.

Stevens, Bonnie Klomp, and Larry L. Stewart. *A Guide to Literary Criticism and Research.* 2nd ed. Fort Worth: Harcourt Brace Jovanovich, 1992.

Stevenson, Lionel. "The Artistic Problem: Science Fiction as Romance." In *SF: The Other Side of Realism.* Ed. Thomas D. Clareson. Bowling Green, Ohio: Bowling Green University Popular Press. 96–104.

Symons, Julian. *Mortal Consequences: A History from the Detective Story to the Crime Novel.* New York: Schocken Books, 1972.

Tharp, Mike. "Popularizing Contempt." *U.S. News and World Report,* 9 March 1992: 50.

Trotsky, Leon. "The Formalist School of Poetry and Marxism." In Adams. 792–799.

Usen, Shelly. "Film from Japan: Reading Between the Lines." *New York Times,* 5 July 1992, sec. 2: 4.

"Voices from Life: Fiction." *Life,* Fall 1986: 333–334.

Wade, Nicholas. "Method and Madness." *New York Times Magazine,* 5 December 1993: 42.

Weintraub, Bernard. "Selling Jurassic: The Film and the Toys." *New York Times,* 14 June 1993: C11.

"White Male Fear." *Economist,* 29 January 1994: 34.

Wilkie, Tom. "*Jurassic Park* and Genetic Fingerprinting Get Novel Prizes." *British Medical Journal* (International), 23 October 1993: 1024–1025.

Wolf, Naomi. *Fire with Fire: The New Female Power and How It Will Change the Twenty-First Century.* New York: Random House, 1993.

Wollen, Peter. "Theme Park Variations." *Sight and Sound,* July 1993: 6–9.

Wyse, Lois. "The Way We Are." *Good Housekeeping,* April 1994: 230.

Index

Index

About the Author

ELIZABETH A. TREMBLEY is Head of General Education at Davenport College in Holland, Michigan. She has published extensively on modern popular and detective fiction. She is coeditor of *It's A Print!: Detective Fiction from Page to Screen* (1994) and of the mystery and detective fiction section of the forthcoming *Encyclopedia of United States Popular Culture.*